God's Ask

Kathleen Queen

Table of Contents

Dedication i

Acknowledgment ii

About the Author iii

Introduction 1

Chapter One: Just Tell Them Thank You 4

Chapter Two: On Adventure with God 22

Chapter Three: Birth of Hope 41

Chapter Four: What's Your Story? 59

Chapter Five: Understanding Misunderstandings.............. 77

Chapter Six: I Am Woman 107

Chapter Seven: It's "Complexicated" 128

Chapter Eight: All That Glitters..................................... 161

Chapter Nine: Dreams Die Hard..................................... 184

Chapter Ten: Eternal Treasure 210

Notes 233

Dedication

To each Soldier, Sailor, Airman or Marine who served in Operation Iraqi Freedom--may you realize that your individual sacrifices were not a waste, but rather made a significant difference in the lives of millions of people.

To message bearers everywhere - trust, obey, and daily cling to the Lover of your soul. The best is yet to come!

Acknowledgment

It is impossible to name the multitude of people who encouraged me to keep writing this story as the years rolled relentlessly on. I am most grateful. In the final weeks, it was the prior knowledge, comprehensive editing capability, and faithful persistence of S. C. Holdsambeck that got me to the elusive finish line. Thanks, Sammy, you are a gentleman and a scholar.

About the Author

Kathy Queen lived and worked in Iraqi Kurdistan from March 2004 until December 2022. She has been involved in different aspects of cross-cultural missions for most of her adult life. Over the years, she has lived and ministered in South America, Asia, Africa, and Europe. She studied journalism at the University of Montana, has a bachelor's in Christian education, and is certified in TESOL and vocational teaching. She is an avid reader and enjoys research and outdoor activities of all kinds.

Introduction

The uniqueness of *GOD'S ASK* is its ordinary "boots on the ground" over-the-long-haul approach. Theory meets real life with a focus on disciple-making and what God is doing in the hearts of the people in Iraqi Kurdistan and beyond, despite the chaotic turmoil and vast changes that define the 21st century. *GOD'S ASK* is a story that longs to be told. It is a book about everyday life on the foreign mission field in the 21st century and the incredible privilege of watching God at work in the most unlikely ways and places, and why effective discipleship takes lasting commitment and sacrificial love.

Often people refer to cross-cultural service as a calling, but that implies a direct, compelling order with immediate consequences and no sense of choice. It also tends to give most believers an easy out: "I just never felt called." But that is not the way God operates. He sacrificed His own Son to show us the way, but the choice is still ours. Instead of a call of compulsion, He asks, often in a slight whisper of loving inquiry.

GOD'S ASK desires to spur thought and prayerful response. This is the story of one message bearer's (Ryan Shaw's new and more accurate term for "missionaries")[1] sincere attempt to carry out the instructions Jesus gave on earth (Matthew 28:18-20) and all that is discovered in the process. It is not intended to provide comprehensive solutions to all the hard questions but rather to encourage people to get involved for themselves and start asking them.

Tiny doors of hope and freedom have been opened in the midst of a very dark land known as the Middle East. It is the ongoing work of the Body of Christ to purposefully walk through those doors with ears wide open, bearing tidings of great joy from Jesus, the only One who brings lasting light and eternal hope to the world. The world is now at a place that demands we cling to the promise that our true citizenship is in heaven regardless of our earthly nationality. For many believing Americans, that is a particularly bitter pill to swallow, but as we watch the country we once knew and still fiercely love continue to divide and weaken irreparably, we must remember that true deliverance lies elsewhere and always has.

The war in Iraq has affected a majority of the American public in at least some small way, and it has deeply affected the families of those who have lost loved ones. Those folks deserve to know that on the other side of the world, their sons and daughters are revered as larger-than-life heroes by people who have literally been at war for decades and lost entire generations.

Further, from a biblical standpoint, interest in the Middle East and its happenings is here to stay. Moreover, the vast technological globalization of the world at large has drastically changed the mission playing field. The scriptural "end game" of making disciples will never change, but worldviews, methodologies, and actual roles must adjust significantly in response.

Many believers express a desire to get personally involved in foreign missions, but they're not sure how to go about it anymore. It is the author's hope that the down-to-earth style of this book will entice future message bearers to take the first step and just answer the knock at the door. Hopefully, the book will also be honest enough to dispel some of the pedestal-placing myths that frequently surround and cause lasting harm in the lives of message bearers. *GOD'S ASK* allows readers to join us on the foreign field and discover for themselves that message bearers are often common people with a heart to serve who suddenly find themselves on an astonishing adventure in Jesus's name.

Chapter One: Just Tell Them Thank You

An Unexpected Attitude of Gratitude.

"You're an American, yes?" the elderly Kurdish shop owner asked, rather than responding to my question about the amount owed. It was March of 2004, and I had just arrived in Iraq a few days earlier.

"Yes, I am," I murmured, slowly nodding in return, puzzled.

His expressive face was ravaged by the years, weathered and heavily lined from having survived the unspeakable. The faded, black and white striped turban atop his head bounced a bit as he nodded eagerly, his eyes focused on some imaginary point behind me to avoid direct visual contact with a woman. His aged hands shook slightly as he enthusiastically began to bag my purchases with a wide, mostly toothless, grin.

"Welcome to Kurdistan then!" he exclaimed, pausing for a moment, and clearing his throat, his hand in an obvious *stop* gesture as he shook his head vigorously at the money I held out. It was obvious from the shack-like state of his small garage store and an abundance of small children calling him "Papa" that he needed every cent.

"No, no, no! I do not want your money. America is our friend now; they have given us a chance." His eyes suddenly seemed to fill with a thousand memories drowned in tears.

With one hand placed solemnly, almost reverently, over his heart, he handed me the bag. "No, missus—no money, just go back and tell Mister Bush thank you. Tell them all thank you. That is all I want…really."

At that, he looked me straight in the eyes for a brief instant, and the spark of hope couched in deep gratitude that I glimpsed there touched my heart deeply. It was the first time I had experienced this reaction in Iraqi Kurdistan, but it would in no way be the last. I walked slowly back down the pothole-filled muddy lane with my bag of "gifts" and a new sense of certainty mixed with a peace I could not explain. The doubts and fears I had wrestled with on the way into this unique locale faded away. It was going to be okay. These were extraordinarily special people, and God obviously had a plan for their lives that He hadn't told me much about yet.

***

Amman, Jordan-- March 8, 2004

"I personally think it's crazy for Americans to get involved in Iraq," the young Jordanian taxi driver announced, waving one hand in the air while the other cradled a cigarette and carelessly guided his vehicle through surging traffic in every direction with horns blaring and brakes squealing. He met my eyes briefly in the rear-view mirror.

"Don't get me wrong—I like Americans…a lot; my sister and several of my cousins live there now. I would like to visit one day. But you know, Iraqis are not like Jordanians. They are savages; really, they needed someone like Saddam Hussein to control them. Before he came along, they were killing each other by the hundreds. I know Saddam did some things—bad things, but really that is all those kinds of people understand. Besides, Saddam was incredibly good to Jordan—he gave us free petrol all the time. Now with the prices we have to pay, it's hard to make a decent living."

His cell phone rang suddenly, and the driver answered in Arabic and became embroiled in a heated discussion just as we pulled up to the hotel. I quickly paid the amount shown on the meter plus tip and hopped out with a wave while he was still on the phone.

My mind replayed that conversation a number of times that day. What was I getting into? I had just landed the day before in Amman, the capital of the Hashemite Kingdom of Jordan, a tiny country that continues to work hard to make a reputable name for itself on the international scale while sharing borders with Israel and Iraq as well as Syria and Saudi Arabia. At the advice of those who had gone before, I was taking a few days to rest there and mentally prepare for my first journey into Iraqi Kurdistan.

Lesson #1 was clear enough. The situation in this perpetually unstable area of the globe was incredibly complicated, and it was quickly becoming apparent that there is nothing cohesive or generalized about the countries or ethnic groups rather casually labeled the "Middle East" by western governments. At that time, the only possible way for a civilian to enter northern Iraq via air was through Baghdad. So bright and early on March 11, 2004, a number of us congregated in the small terminal of Markka Municipal Airport in Amman for what would become the standard "hurry up and wait" game that any traveler in this part of the world learns to play often, if not patiently. Handwritten tickets repeated manual weigh-ins, and a multitude of seemingly random questions are the norm. Usually, in the end, though, smiles appear as all is well and the time to board eventually arrives.

That day we were flying with Air Serv International, the first civilian air operator granted access to Iraq in 2003 following the end of initial U.S. combat operations. Since there were no flight attendants or working bathrooms on board, the pilot himself took the time beforehand to brief us on the flight plan and standard emergency procedures. He also carefully explained the required spiral landing and takeoff method in effect for all Iraqi air space.

Sure enough, two hours after leaving Jordan, our small 17-seat prop plane began the mandatory corkscrew dive into Baghdad International Airport. Actually, before I had even left the States, I had heard much "reassurance" about this special spiral landing maneuver designed to fool and avoid any heat-seeking missiles that might be aimed our way. Still, my over-active imagination had me well prepared for a stomach-lurching, tilt-a-whirl ride in the sky when, in reality, I was pleasantly surprised.

It was more like being a bug on the inside of a blender's shake canister going in slow motion, actually gentle enough for one to get a brief, "rounded" look at the infamous Baghdad or "Sackpapa" airport, as its code name became in casual correspondence. Clear signs of the war abounded, with assorted burnt-out objects, large tanks, manned guard towers, barbed wire, and dirt bunkers in plain view as we approached. Unexpectedly though, it was decidedly greener than I anticipated, and there was also visible evidence of a totally different time, with spacious palm tree-lined boulevards, park areas, and elaborate mansions surrounded by beautifully designed waterscapes still standing in the distance.

Disembarking from the plane, we stood as a little group on the mammoth tarmac in order to identify our own luggage when it came off. The whole place was vacant except for the well-armed soldiers that kept appearing out of nowhere. Our seasoned South African pilots were obviously relaxed and joking with one another about their next vacation days, but the rest of us felt oddly vulnerable in the bright sunlight with machine guns all around. Almost as one, we hurried to the relative safety of the empty terminal.

In retrospect, it went way beyond empty. It was like visiting an international ghost airport and gave me an eerie sense of unease that had those little hairs on the back of my neck standing at strict attention. I even felt a chill climb my spine as I glanced at the immense flight board on the wall above and saw that it was still listing the expected arrivals and departures for a long-ago date in 2003—just prior to the start of Operation Iraqi Freedom.

We were the only visitors that day in this immense building, obviously designed to aptly handle thousands of harried, prospective passengers simultaneously. The few security staff present seemed to have just woken up from a long nap in order to deal with us. Most of the lights remained off while we were there, and every movement or voice directive echoed loudly while we watched our luggage slowly reappear on the squeaky conveyor belt of one of the multitudes of carousels that lined the back wall. After a cursory manual search and another round of questions, we were all herded back onto our aircraft for the journey north.

As we reversed the strange circular motion and smoothly straightened out, I watched both the Tigris and Euphrates Rivers become mere ribbons in the vast desert landscape below. The constant roar of the engines effectively discouraged idle conversation, and my mind soon wandered back to how this particular adventure had all begun.

April 1, 2003—Colorado USA

"Do you want to go to Iraq?"

I first heard that question nonchalantly posed over the telephone one morning by my boss. The war had just gotten underway, and the eyes of the world were focused there on a daily basis. In America, the horrific tragedy and far-reaching implications of the 9/11 attack were still fresh in everyone's minds. I think just about every U.S. citizen over a certain age can respond with a detailed answer to the query, *"Where were you the morning the planes hit the World Trade Center?"*

As so often used to happen in the midst of great pain and calamity, our entire country pulled together in a way that I had never seen for myself before, though I had heard stories from my grandparents. Hanging chads and party politics were all but forgotten. Many young men and women changed career paths and enlisted in the military. Churches across the country reported a revival of interest in spiritual matters and getting things "right" with God. It was a piercing wake-up call, and our nation seemed to listen…at least for a while.

Thus, the question that morning was unexpected but not completely shocking. Even though that particular discussion quickly dissolved into the usual banter of daily office life, the question itself remained behind to prick both my heart and imagination at the oddest times. Further discussions with the president of our small mission revealed that he too sensed God's leading in what appeared at first to be a random, if not downright bizarre, idea. Thus, the research began in earnest and persisted in my spare moments as God continued to murmur, *"Will you?"* Before long, I realized that my response, flavored by a certain sense of urgency, was clear and growing more insistent. "Yes, Lord, send me ... please."

I was 42 years old and in the sad midst of rebuilding my life as a newly divorced person. Through a series of unexpected "Goddities," I had been offered a job as an Executive Assistant for the President of Entrust, a small, historically covert Christian mission organization now based in Colorado. Originally known as Biblical Education by Extension International (BEE), Entrust was first founded as a cooperative effort of several large well-known missions that met together in Vienna, Austria, in 1979 to address the ongoing need for equipping inexperienced pastors and lay leaders behind the impenetrable Iron Curtain.[2]

My own passion for foreign missions first ignited in the summer of 1991 when I was privileged to help lead a Teen Missions International team of 24 youth on a tough work project to a remote village in Sumatra, Indonesia. The incredible spiritual and physical needs that I witnessed there changed the emphasis of my life going forward. For weeks, our team braved the oppressive, humid heat of the island and various virulent diseases to hike several miles up a steep incline each day in order to lay PVC pipe to bring clean water from a high mountain spring to the villages below.

At the time, it was estimated that over 60 percent of the Indonesian children in the area under the age of five were dying from contaminated water. Sadly, the villagers had never connected the dots regarding the cause, and many believed the local witch doctor's verdict that the deaths were due to tribal curses and angry spirits. That summer, the residents repeatedly voiced their astonishment that American and Canadian teenagers would come so far at their own expense and work incredibly hard without complaint for people they had never met. In the end, not only did the project succeed, but it actually inspired the villagers themselves to take over after we left and add pipes to get the water to even more areas. Most importantly, it gave our team the right to be heard, as night after night the grateful residents and officials turned out to hear what the kids had to say about the living water of Jesus Christ.

Subsequent mission experiences in other parts of Indonesia, South America, and Africa only served to fan the flame within. Thus, when I began to sense the "go" nudge once again regarding Iraq, I have to admit that my primary emotion was one of glad expectation. There is just nothing on this earth that compares with the privilege of watching God at work in the midst of otherwise hopeless circumstances!

Truthfully, involvement in missions is much like a chronic ailment that never quite goes away. I am convinced that it's one "illness" that every follower is meant to catch in one way or another. Look closely at the words of Jesus on the Mount of Ascension:

> *God authorized and commanded me to commission you: Go out and train everyone you meet, far and near, in this way of life, marking them by baptism in the threefold name: Father, Son, and Holy Spirit. Then instruct them in the practice of all I have commanded you. I'll be with you as you do this, day after day after day, right up to the end of the age.*   Matthew 28:18-20 (MSG)

His ongoing orders are clear and simple—especially considering the overarching promise of companionship that He is offering! Despite many rumors to the contrary, foreign mission service is not and has never been an elitist club for highly gifted super saints. Look around or look at me—God continues to delight in taking ordinary people on extraordinary journeys of faith and dependence where, out of calamitous necessity, life suddenly becomes all about Him.

Further, from Moses to David to Jesus himself, God's Word repeatedly points out that those whom mortal men would never even consider are the very ones that God chooses first. He just wants teachable servant hearts willing to trust Him to do the hard part. Rest assured that the concept of missions is not about God needing our assistance. After all, He is God and, therefore, completely capable of finishing the task any way He chooses. Instead, it is out of His incredible love for each one of us that He invites us to utterly engage with Him and become a part of something much bigger than ourselves.

Isn't it amazing that in our abundantly blessed, fully automated, industrialized American society, where everything is essentially all about self-indulgence, we seem to have lost much of our passion for living? The gift of life itself is no longer even very compelling. If it were, I doubt the abortion rate would be near the tragic numbers that are currently in the U.S. Yet God's own unchanging, ever-fervent nature is evident in every single facet of His creation—a creation that we get to share with Him forever. Jesus promised trouble in this broken world of ours but assures us it is a temporary condition meant for our own eternal growth.

May 2003—Colorado USA

Admittedly, it is one thing to believe that God is calling you to serve Him in a place like Iraq; it is an entirely different matter, however, to convince others of that notion and then find a feasible means of actually getting there. First, I had to locate a legitimate umbrella under which I could enter the country and try to be of some service. It also needed to be a situation where I would be able to get to know the believers in the area and, over time, assess the current need for and feasibility of Entrust-type training. From the Lord's perspective, it is always all about the journey, and that is one lesson that automatically goes against the grain of a task-oriented society like ours. I have often wondered how Jesus felt during the 30 years prior to the advent of his public ministry. God's timing is paramount, and He does not seem to care what you put in your day timer.

In the end, it took me six months of searching and knocking on lots of doors that just would not budge or eventually slammed shut. Slowly it became apparent that, if I were going to get in at all, it would probably be in the northern no-fly region of the country where a people known as Kurds had worked tirelessly over the preceding decade to create a safe haven of sorts.

The majority of this people group lives in a geographical

area that you will not find designated on most any official map, though it is an area that can now be described by more and more historians. It basically takes a "bite" out of the relatively new border designations of Turkey, Iran, Syria, and Iraq. Kurds currently number over 30 million people in that general area. They comprise the largest ethnic group in the world that has never had its own nation-state, despite the fact that such has been promised to them numerous times throughout history. Kurds are neither Arabs nor Persians. Actually, they themselves believe, and many scholars concur, that they are direct descendants of the ancient Medes mentioned numerous times in the Bible.[3]

For decades, the Kurds of Iraq have been ruled by hatred, horrifying Machiavellian oppression, and the ever-present threat of total annihilation. Until recent years, they have rarely been allowed to think for themselves, much less lead others. Suddenly circumstances in northern Iraq thrust them into a pivotal political role, almost without warning. Though history's jury is still out in terms of a final verdict, there is much to be gleaned by studying the chronological "big picture" of the Kurds. Fortunately, much more material is available on the subject now than when I first began researching in 2003. One of the best-detailed reads regarding the general history up to the ISIS conflict can be found in the 2014 release, *The Miracle of the Kurds: A Remarkable Story of Hope Reborn in Northern Iraq* by Stephen Mansfield.

Frustrating as the wait was at the time, it was well spent in prayer and preparation. Once I actually started working with believers in Iraqi Kurdistan, I began to realize just how fitting my previous research assignments for Entrust had been. One of my first jobs at the headquarters was to assist in the creation of a deputation and recruitment video. After years of purposefully flying under the radar to carry on training in closed Communist countries, the whole organization was faced with a paradigm shift. We needed a marketing tool that would help prospective donors and staff to "see" what it is we do and, we hoped, to encourage further funding and more workers for leadership training and discipleship efforts where we felt God leading.

Without question, the Lord is on the move in some of the most unlikely places these days, and new believers are multiplying at an astounding rate in areas all over the globe. Certainly, that is incredibly wonderful news, but it does not in any way negate His clear mandate to each and every believer to follow His own example and disciple well those whom He brings into the Kingdom.

Unfortunately, purposeful discipleship and leadership training are not particularly easy visuals to create. In the end, we spent significant time dissecting and envisioning what was meant by the idea of the "infant" church. Like much of modern "Christianese," it's familiar terminology—but if it is an accurate analogy of believers and societies who are young in the Lord, then what does that mean when it comes to the comprehensive equipping of the saints?

In scripture, God often uses physical birth to describe the process of spiritual awakening.[4] In many ways, new believers are as vulnerable and essentially helpless as newborn babies. It is a day-in and day-out progression that is very demanding and time-consuming and sometimes does not seem to be making any real progress. Yet eventually, by the grace of God, babies grow up and may even raise babies themselves.

We ended up using that simple analogy in an introduction video to present the crucial and ongoing need for nurturing, consistent discipleship that stays the course—despite the ever-present challenges of astounding growth rates and inaccessible, often treacherous places. When I arrived in Kurdistan, the same correlation came to life in ways I never expected. Theoretical discussion suddenly became a real-life challenge. Bottom line: if we love Him, we will feed his sheep—wherever they are, just like He said.[5]

November 2003—Colorado USA

It was astounding how fast everything moved once the Lord opened the right door. It was late November, and I had just returned from our yearly staff development conference in Hungary. Anyone who has jumped the "pond" for themselves and made that 8 to10-hour time zone leap knows about jet lag. Your body wants to sleep at the oddest times, and your mind seems to swirl in a perpetual funk. Thus, one night around 3:00 AM, I was surfing on the web, casually looking for any new developments in the "want-to-go-to-Iraq" saga, when I stumbled upon an ad for teacher trainers in a place called Sulaymaniyah, Iraq. Before long, I was on my way to Tennessee to meet with Servant Group International (SGI), a young mission with a big heart to help the Iraqi Kurds.

What happens when people pray? I am quite sure that all of us have been deeply touched at one time or another by incredible stories that answer that very question in the most astounding ways. Such is the case in the history I was given of three small English-speaking classical elementary schools in Kurdistan, Iraq. It all started in the early 1990s when the congregation of an independent community church in Nashville, Tennessee, decided that they were going to covenant together to pray often and regularly for the Kurdish people who had been so victimized by so many for so long.

Then "Desert Storm" commenced, and this body of believers kept praying. Not too long after that, they began receiving word that hundreds of Iraqi Kurdish refugees were coming to America—to Nashville, as a matter of fact. That same church body continued to pray and actively minister and introduce Jesus to those refugees. As time passed, some of these new Iraqi believers felt led to return and share Jesus in their homeland, and it was not surprising that they asked their American friends and mentors to pray about coming with them to help. Essentially, out of those prayers, Servant Group International was born and placed its first team of three American workers in northern Iraq in 1993.

As churches sprang up and believers multiplied in the relatively calm no-fly zone of Northern Iraq, Servant Group began partnering with local government officials and one segment of national church leadership to help establish Classical Christian schools. Their first school opened in early 2001; an English-based curriculum was employed, and indigenous teachers were trained and monitored by expatriate staff.

Since I had a background in youth work and education, my job was to serve as one of those trainers for several months while I got acquainted with the area and began to research and appraise overall leadership training needs among the area house churches. In some ways, it felt like being drafted! A sense of both certainty and resolve became my constant companion.

Chapter Two: On Adventure with God

Rocking the Cradle of Civilization

March 2004--Hawler (Irbil), Iraq

As the plane touched down, it almost seemed like we were landing in an abandoned corn field that had somehow produced a small runway amid the tall, spindly weeds. The co-pilot warned us, as we taxied to a stop, to put away all cameras and keep them stowed until we left the airport grounds, which were considered classified coalition property. The Irbil "airport" at that time consisted of a two-room wooden outpost-type shack...and nothing else. Immediately, the most important thing on everyone's mind was that someone was there to meet them. It was obviously a long walk to anywhere, and once again, all those milling about seemed to possess some type of scary-looking automatic weapon.

In those days, an American passport was a sure ticket to red carpet treatment in the north, no matter what or who you were. Hence, all of us fortunate U.S. citizens were welcomed immediately in a friendly, respectful way and quickly released to the other side of a tall chain link fence where our various rides awaited. It was with great relief that I quickly spotted a familiar face in the form of K, a striking young American lady who had been a part of the orientation I attended in Nashville, which also happened to be her hometown. A successful free-lance photographer with a heart of gold and a burning desire to serve the Lord with her talents, she had come at her own expense to make an orientation and recruitment video for future staff of Servant Group. Beside her stood F, a well-dressed, broad-shouldered, young Kurd with a large dark bushy mustache that might have been frightening if one did not also notice straight away the genuine warmth in his eyes and the brightness of his smile. *"Welcome to Kurdistan, my sister,"* he said softly. It was one of those "Goddity" moments where my spirit bore witness with his—a rather strange sensation referred to in scripture[6] that only fellow believers can begin to understand. I just knew without a doubt that this man was my spiritual brother and that the God we both served had some incredibly special plans in store for his life.

F quickly loaded up my gear into the trunk of an immaculately kept late-model Mercedes, and within a few minutes, we were off, only to stop for lunch at a popular little café when we reached the town center. I immediately noticed, as we entered the restaurant, that K and I were the only females in sight, and the various clusters of men stopped talking and stared as we went by. It is one of those experiences that you never really get used to, but eventually, you learn to accept what you cannot change.

Then it was a quick trip to the single bathroom for an immediate "feet-on" refresher course in eastern toilets. Such are referred to among friends as squatty potties since they consist of a white, starter block ridged basin with a tiled hole in the ground and a faucet nearby for cleanup. As a lifelong Charmin & friends' fan, I have yet to master the whole drench and drip-dry approach. Thus, I have always appreciated that it's common practice in the restaurants of Kurdistan to have a box of tissue on every table, as that is not usually an item found in any form in the bathroom itself.

Following a delicious lunch of kebab and hummus, we drove on through town, and I was immediately captivated by the chaotic traffic rules or lack thereof. It has improved tremendously in the last few years, but at that time, it was basically one giant game of "chicken"—or blind man's bluff depending on your perspective. I was also impressed by the number of people and animals on the streets, the number of firearms visible, and the mix of muted western and traditional clothing. Again, the vast majority of those out in public were male and under the age of thirty. As time went by, I would get used to feeling "old" since Iraqi Kurdistan is a young entity in more ways than one. As of the last census, over 50% of its population is under the age of twenty and only 4% are over 63. The ethnic demographic is also surprisingly diverse. Though the majority of Kurdistan's population is, in fact, Kurdish, there are also significant numbers of Assyrians, Chaldeans, Turkmen, Armenians, and ever-increasing numbers of Arabs scattered throughout the region.[7]

As is true with many objects in Kurdistan, the struggle for dominance is frequently found in official language choices. Hence, there are often two names for a city or place–the Kurdish name and the Arabic equivalent. Take for instance, the capital of the region. Generally, it is known as Erbil or Arbil or Irbil since proper spelling and transliteration of either language into English also becomes a constant problem because of the widely differing scripts. However, the Kurds, by and large, refer to the same town by its Kurdish name, Hawler (how-lair). In fact, when the first version of the fancy new international airport went up in 2005, I snapped a picture of the professional sign over the doors proclaiming to all: *"Welcome to Hawler International Airport,"* only to find that the next time I was there, the same sign had magically become: *"Welcome to Irbil International Airport"*…and, so it goes—a struggle for identity that comes in waves and never quite disappears.

Whatever its name, at that time, the town was yet to be the bustling big city, emerging tourist destination, and recognized thriving capital of the new Kurdistan Regional Government(KRG) that it is today. Instead, it was still evidently reeling from a devasting explosion that had taken place the previous month in the immediate area. Several important Kurdish officials from both of their main parties were killed in a suicide bomber attack on central government buildings. The tragedy also served as the final impetus for all of the UN staff to abandon the whole area for a time. The entire matter was a frequent topic of public discussion and debate for the first few months that I lived in Kurdistan, and it was often referred to as one of the cementing links between the Kurds and the Americans in terms of the sides that were drawn. War correspondent Mike Tucker, who was also in the country during that time, reported:

> A long-time friend and comrade of General Zebari, the deeply respected peshmerga commander Sami Abdul Rahman, was among the 110 Kurds murdered in Hawler on February 1, 2004. After the Hawler terrorist bombing, imams (Muslim clerics) in Mosul, the Ba'athist stronghold of northern Iraq, preached the following in their Friday sermons throughout February 2004, according to Kurdish military intelligence and Adnan Barwari, a Kurdish activist and translator who was in Mosul during that same time: "Praise the death of the Kurds! The martyrdom operations are joyous! Kill the Kurds; they are dogs and jackals and thieves! When you kill a Kurd, you will receive the

same treasure from Allah as when you kill an American soldier! Kill the Kurds and kill the American soldiers![8]

***

March 2004--Sulaymaniyah, Iraq

After lunch, we drove on to Sulaymaniyah, which at the time was about an hour and a half away. Soon after, it became well over two hours since it was no longer safe to go through the city of Kirkuk. The regional government has always been serious about maintaining its outstanding safety record, especially regarding the internationals. So, when a hot spot such as Mosul or Kirkuk became a threat, the standard *modus operandi* was to build a new road around the problem. "It might take longer, but you will get there" was the traditional explanation.

From day one, I was fascinated with and somewhat taken aback by the people of the area. Unlike the outspoken, frequently angry outbursts that I had witnessed in other parts of the Middle East, the people of Kurdistan had a gentle demeanor and an aura of vulnerability that was nearly tangible. Once they got over that initial sense of shyness, they were almost always friendly and warm, ready to practice their English and express their appreciation for the chance to live their lives in hope rather than the ominous shadow of a tyrannical madman who was indeed determined to annihilate the entire Kurdish race.[9]

Admittedly, years of virtual non-involvement officially, as well as the advent of ISIS and the United States' extremely strange role as a country at its inception, have weakened this attitude of gratitude, and with good reason. Yet you can still find, especially among the common people, those who consider Americans as family and always will, no matter what. This is not to say that life was/is particularly easy in Kurdistan even now. They continue to struggle with abhorrent corruption and a near-ground-zero infrastructure, particularly in outlying areas. To be sure, it is sometimes hard to believe that it used to be a lush land teeming with growth and production. The whole area has been repeatedly destroyed and chemically poisoned in the last several decades of ongoing conflict, and it still shows, especially in the more rural areas.

The inexperienced administration wrestles continually with many issues typical of third-world thinking. For instance, power outages are a constant annoyance, especially when the backup to the backup generator breaks down as well. Everyone seems to feel like it is someone else's responsibility to solve the problem, and no one appears to actually be doing much about it when it comes to long-range planning.

In the spring, you hear about the regional government's intention to "stockpile" as much as possible to keep the coolers running in the summer, yet in the summer, you hear that control has suddenly been switched to the government in Baghdad. For the most part, people just laugh and shake their heads. The Kurds are true survivors. Their basic pragmatic, optimistic outlook and a general sense of camaraderie extend to one and all, remaining fairly positive no matter what the hardships. They simply get on with life, whatever that might look like at any given moment.

As I think back to that first term in Kurdistan, I am reminded of how amazing it was to be there during that particular time in history. I soon came to realize that it was much easier just to be a part of daily life on the edge of a war zone, than to be in the U.S. wondering about what I was going through, with CNN footage as one's constant frame of reference.

At that time, I lived with four other SGI staff in a nice, enormous house in a quiet neighborhood, not far from the elementary school where we all worked. Below are some of the first "knee" mails I wrote to my friends and supporters back home a few weeks after my initial arrival. Unreal as it might sound, daily life in Kurdistan in 2004 was full of surprises and often just plain fun.

March 18, 2004

Hi Dear Friends—

Greetings and Salutations from the heart of Kurdistan!

I am continually convinced that you all, as my beloved prayer battalion, have by far the tougher job in this unique adventure. While you are bombarded by the negative and tragic events of war and terrorism in this incredible land, I am strategically planning occasional "squatty potty" avoidance tactics or how six people will each successfully obtain a hot shower on less than three hours of power a day or laughing at the antics of a third grader playing his first ever game of baseball.

I don't have angry people telling me I shouldn't be here and demanding that I leave immediately—instead, I have them teaching me Kurdish, inviting me to tea (at least 3x a day), and kissing each cheek repeatedly, both coming and going. In short, I must admit, I'm having a blast (not literally, of course), and God graciously affirms each day in numerous ways that I'm where He wants me to be. I do feel safe, and we are all trying to be wise in terms of security and alertness. So, thanks for your prayers—keep them coming and try not to worry.

As a group, we were saddened and greatly grieved to learn of the recent hideous attack and murder of four American missionaries outside Mosul (approximately three hours away) but on the one hand, that could mean we are doing something very right, and the evil bully types are trying to stop it with desperate fear tactics. Mosul is right outside the Kurdistan border, and lingering hostilities are much more evident. The event actually happened within days of the anniversary of Halabja—a community that lies right on the Iraq/Iran border that was indiscriminately bombed by Saddam with a mixture of mustard gas and napalm several years ago to prove a point of control and "get rid of some Kurds." Over five thousand men, women & children died instantly, and hundreds more live with the debilitating and crippling effects yet today. The pictures are sobering and clear evidence of a people that refuse to give up hope despite unimaginable oppression.

> *Therefore, we do not lose heart. Even though our outward man is perishing, the inward man is being renewed day by day. For our light affliction, which is but for a moment, is working for us a far more exceeding and eternal weight of glory, while we do not look at the things which are seen, but at the things which are not seen. For the things which are seen are temporary, but the things which are not seen are eternal.*

> 2 Corinthians 4:16-18 (NKJV)

March 25, 2004

Let me try to answer two of your most popular questions:

<u>Weather:</u> Well, when I first got here, and many of you were telling me about GREAT days with temps in the 60s & 70s back home—what's known as "the black wind" had arrived, and suddenly there was snow on the mountain peaks, and temperatures plummeted to the low 40s accompanied by a strong biting wind that blew 24 hours a day for six days. With the advent of Newroz (Kurdish New Year = first day of spring) this past weekend, though, the wind died, the sun came out, and it's been beautiful. I am told it is basically only green in Iraq for this one month of the year, so we are all savoring it.

<u>Food:</u> speaking of Newroz—the usual tradition is to celebrate by going on a picnic, and three of us were invited to go with the family of one of our teachers. The day started bright and early (6:30 AM) in hopes of beating some of the traffic to the mountains—however, we did not really succeed on that particular note. After all, gas only costs about 6 cents a gallon at the moment, and abandoned cars are in abundance, so traffic jams are a common occurrence. Anyway, it took us a few extra hours, but we finally got to a great place on a lake and the mother of the clan we were with immediately whipped out the makings for tea, and we had fresh hot wheat "buns" with yogurt, cheese, and two types of honey comb (meal one). Then we hiked a bit and had a

little more tea, flat bread and some oranges and bananas (meal two). Soon after, we got our first lesson in Kurdish dancing—it's sort of a two-step, shoulder shrug line dance deal that is pretty easy to fake and provides lots of entertaining exercise which is most helpful in digesting all the copious amounts of food. This was followed by a buffet lunch of flat bread, hummus, boiled lamb, olives, bite-sized grape leaves stuffed with a rice and yogurt mixture seasoned with onion and dill, gargantuan green beans that are actually cooked in their pods, and a large bowl of salad fixings with enough forks for everyone including the neighbors to dig in (meal three). This was followed shortly by fresh mint sprigs, tea and a humongous piece of yellow cake with bananas between the layers & frosted with chocolate flakes and rich syrup (meal four). Then it was more dancing and off for a stroll to the lake and a short boat ride. After the "wash up," a brief rest, another hike, pinecone & wildflower collecting and yet another round of dancing before we fired up the "barbecue" for a literal feast of chicken and lamb kabobs served with more flat bread, fruit and lettuce and tomato sprayed with orange juice, accompanied by soda pop and tea (meals 5 and 6). We continued to munch on this fare throughout the evening as we danced, sang, chatted with the neighbors, and enjoyed watching the stars appear in the evening sky. All of the aforementioned items are fairly typical Kurdish cuisine, although thankfully, not normally served all on the same day. Suffice to say, in the end, a grand time was had by all and it definitely gave new meaning to the term "picnic."

<u>*Prayer Requests:*</u>

That people here continue to daily meet & accept Jesus

The school gains favor in the eyes of the transitional government

We are an effective support of and encouragement to the growing infant church

Unity among the international Christians in the area

Continued opportunities for the witness to the various American military Health and safety

May 11, 2004

Hi All!

This past month has flown by, and I still cannot believe that it is already May. Although, admittedly, the ever-increasing temperature here is an obvious reminder that summer cometh—ready or not. I just keep thinking that I will sit down and dash off a 'day-in-the-life' of type epistle to you all, but every day seems so unique unto itself that it kind of becomes a never-ending saga in my mind.

For instance, at the moment, I am developing Math, Science and Geography finals for all six grades. It's actually kind of fun and a great refresher course on all that "stuff" I used to know way back when. On the downside, my brain is now in a rather unique funk; lost for the moment somewhere between the concept of properly diagramming the correct placement of effort, load and fulcrum for all three classes of levers—and orally quizzing a six-year-old on "what is a push?" and "what is a pull?"

Just about the time I really get focused, it seems that something completely unique to life here erupts, and the best-laid plans of yours truly are literally out the window. The other day it was your basic worldview crisis in the girls' bathroom. Unbeknownst to any of us, a pigeon had quietly decided to build her nest behind the water tank in the corner of one empty stall. All was well until hatch day, and then, of course, the sound of the newborns attracted a group of fourth-grade girls to investigate more closely. Among them was one of our staff's kids who tried to "pet" one of the chicks, and things rapidly deteriorated from that point. The Kurdish kids solemnly declared that she was bound to burn in Hell since she was now unclean. It is those kinds of moments that truly make you want to laugh and cry at the same time.

Meanwhile, I continue to be amazed by story after story of remarkable conversion in the heart of this Islamic land. I am helping a group of ladies (part are believers and part are not) from the school with their English and my Kurdish by translating the Gospel of John together once a week. One of them, C, shared her testimony last week.

She and her husband, T, had been married about eight years when he unexpectedly accepted Jesus as his Savior after one of those "western foreigner-types" from the outside had befriended him and shared the Gospel. At first, they separated at her insistence, as she wanted no part of his new life and the family turmoil and persecution that went with it. For four years, she watched from a distance as he continued to live a completely changed life and provide for the family financially. He often let her know that he prayed every day for her and their daughter to come back to him and find Jesus too.

The tears started flowing as she whispered that God had answered those very prayers three years ago. Her devout Muslim family immediately shunned her, and shortly after her own conversion, her younger brother showed up at her house with a loaded gun which he proceeded to hold to her head, declaring in a drunken rage that if she did not renounce Jesus once and for all, he would pull the trigger. Gazing right into his eyes without flinching, she put her hand around the muzzle of the gun and said— "Go ahead and shoot then as I will never renounce the Son of the Living God," and with that, still looking at him, she put the end of the gun in her mouth. The brother dropped the weapon with a sob and ran from the house. Those kinds of stories are fairly common here and serve as a potent reminder of the price that has been paid and the high stakes at hand.

On that same note, after a number of foiled attempts, we have finally succeeded in borrowing some projection equipment and a copy of "The Passion of the Christ," and we have invited quite a crowd over to the house for a showing this Thursday afternoon. Please feel free to bathe this whole endeavor with much prayer.

In Him Who is Able to do abundantly above all that we ask or think, kq

P.S.—and here's a little sample of Kurdish translation— remember it reads from right to left, so a typical spelling test is sort of akin to a head-on collision.

Love,   Thoughts   &   خۆشتۆويستى،باوةرِمانـ، نوێذةكانمان
—Prayers

There were several special experiences that first term that did not even make it into letters. In situations like that, you are so busy living life each day that you sometimes forget to process the meaning of it all. It did not really feel like a war zone, but there were subtle signs of such. At times, we would suddenly get warned to stay inside and off the streets. Additionally, we tried to be conscientious of varying our routes and checking for bombs under a vehicle before getting in. We also paid close attention to the advice of local believers and resident US military, although it was tricky when such advice differed radically. It all seemed a bit surreal since we felt so loved, protected and safe, but we knew that it could change for the worse in the blink of an eye. Troops on patrol were also a fairly common sight at that point—both Coalition and Peshmerga.

The Peshmerga are a fascinating breed. They are the Kurdish Freedom Fighters of old (both men and women) and now make up the primary national military force of Kurdistan. The term Peshmerga literally means "one who faces death." Moreover, their experience with guerrilla fighting and winning against all odds is a historical fact. As far as the Kurds are concerned, they have already been at war for decades and thus remained a bit bewildered in those days, both by our western references to how long Operation Iraqi Freedom was taking and our seeming lack of interest in their experience and advice.

Certainly, there were personnel struggles and conflicts in unexpected places as well. Sorry, that part of life does not change, no matter where you are. In God's eyes, it is all about the *process*, remember? Whether we like it or not, it is evidently what He was thinking when He designed salvation so that our various quirks and fallibilities remain firmly in place even after we become His kid!

Why can't you be more like me, anyway? The worst of it is that I think many sincere message bearers get completely blindsided when the inevitable happens. They are so confident that things will be different once they are actually on the mission field—surely, all interpersonal and character challenges will magically disappear, never to be seen again. That particular fairy tale must go hand in hand with the ever-popular missionary super-saint myth.

Dear reader, you may be eagerly wondering if I am going to share all the juicy details of those tough times. Nope, I never have liked reality shows. I understand and empathize with your sense of curiosity, but to be honest, it would not serve any constructive purpose. In the end, it is not that much different from the yucky trials and tribulations you yourself go through at times with your family, job, church, or home group. It is called life in a fallen world. On the field, it is just tremendously magnified, and you occasionally come under friendly fire or even launch an arsenal of your own at the wrong targets.

As part of their preparation for the field, Teen Missions International teaches that there are five "Ds" of the devil that a message bearer needs to constantly watch out for: Division, Distraction, Defeat, Despondency and Discouragement. I have personally seen them all used effectively, sometimes disastrously, anywhere there is a body of believers that gathers together. It is easy to get the overall picture of Kurdistan in focus when you add to that familiar mix the challenge of incredible cultural differences along with heavy doses of spiritual warfare. Then top it all off with the daily uncertainty of life on the brink of a war zone where absolutely everything is in a state of constant transition. All of one's own peculiarities and weaknesses become glaringly evident in that kind of stretching fishbowl.

Moreover, the Lord delights in revealing our vulnerabilities to us as His strength is made perfect in our weakness. It is sad that, as believers, we work so hard to deny that truth to ourselves and, more notably, to each other. It's all about the outlook, as CS Lewis so aptly states:

> If you think of this world as a place simply
> intended for our happiness, you find it quite
> intolerable: think of it as a place for training
> and correction, and it's not so bad.[10]

How true. Earthly life is temporary and needs to be viewed as God's own basic training. When we cannot see His hand, we must trust His heart, and by His priceless grace, we might even grab a glimpse of heaven along the way!

Chapter Three: Birth of Hope

Joy Unspeakable

In those early years, it was truly as if God was allowing us all to witness the actual birth of hope in an entire region, and we knew we were privileged to be there for such a distinctive time. If you, too, are a *Chronicles of Narnia* fan, it was very much akin to the illustration of spring finally coming to the land and the delight of every creature when the icy dark bleakness of winter was at last dispelled, and all of creation was born anew!

Have you ever watched a live birth? Any delivery is awe-inspiring, but unquestionably, human birth is the pinnacle of miracles to witness. Despite the obvious pain and general ambiguity, the moment when you gaze upon that tiny creation of life is filled with a sense of wonder that goes far beyond words. Perhaps that is why God, in His infinite wisdom, chose to deliver the astonishingly good news of eternal salvation in just that manner. The advent of Jesus' time on earth could have been arranged in any number of astounding ways. The fact that God chose an obscure young peasant girl to give Him birth in the normal fashion is a beautiful portrait of the value He places on family relationships and the inherent joy of such, even in the most difficult of conditions.

***

To be honest, I am usually reticent about mentioning the life and death of my own infant son, Johnathan. No matter how carefully I phrase it, it always seems to be painful for the listener. There is just something about the death of a baby that twists people's hearts inside out. But, as always, to see God at work, you have to get beyond the pain. Not to say that my own heart was not contorted with grief and anger at the time, as a miraculous pregnancy suddenly began to unravel. I had always suffered from severe endometriosis and resulting infertility. After 12 years of marriage, we had all but given up on that issue. Besides, I had been granted the gift of three incredible step-kids whom I had grown to deeply love and pray for as my own.

Further, it was the fall of 1991, and we had just moved to Florida, having joined the staff of Teen Missions International a year prior. We were eager to serve God in faraway places. Then suddenly, I was pregnant. To be honest, I was cocky, and so were my close friends in claiming that, though my body began to send out warning signals almost immediately, surely this baby was a special miracle from God and was going to be fine, no matter what. Unfortunately, it turned out that God's actual idea of "fine" and my own were polar opposites.

The real trouble began at about nineteen weeks of gestation. I suddenly experienced sharp abdominal pains that were originally diagnosed as Braxton Hicks contractions, but a closer look determined I actually had an incompetent cervix (a lovely name any mother-to-be never wants to hear) and had begun to dilate. In simple layman's terms, it means that the oven door unexpectedly pops open when the "cake" is half done. So, I immediately became a high-risk crisis pregnancy and was rushed a few hours away to a neonatal hospital in West Palm Beach.

At that point, events became quite a blur as I was hooked up to several machines at once, and various medications were administered in hopes of stopping labor. I do vaguely remember a few bouts of extreme vomiting in the ambulance ride down that was later determined to be an allergic reaction to one of those meds. Unfortunately, the force of the vomiting was so intense that it blew a small hole in my womb. Thus, I arrived in West Palm with two problems—I was partially dilated and now leaking amniotic fluid.

I will always have tremendous respect and gratitude for those incredible people who staff neonatal departments and press on heroically against tremendous odds. Without delay, they put me on 24/7 bed rest with my head down and my abdomen up as they tried valiantly to plug the hole and add fluid back into the womb. For one solid month, it worked, and I grew quite close to the dedicated staff whom I saw daily. Then one morning, the feared infection arrived with a vengeance that would kill us both if immediate action were not taken.

Johnathan was a one lb. 13 oz, 23-week-old preemie born by c-section on April 22, 1992. He lived/suffered for five days. Preemies themselves are soldiers, too, as their own little lives are often full of pain. Johnathan actually looked like a tiny, wizened old man. His personal doctor introduced himself the morning of Johnathan's delivery and explained that with a micro preemie like Johnathan was considered to be, much seemed to depend on the baby's own desire to fight to live. This same doctor returned four days later with tears in his eyes. A massive brain bleed had begun that night, and the end was inevitably near. He went on to explain that our son didn't fit the normal mode and had surprised all the doctors and nurses as he fought so incredibly hard and still lost…or did he? In that time period, two nurses met Jesus, and my own life was transformed forever, especially as I meditated on earthly death being a beginning rather than an ending.

I was given a chance to share this same narrative and reconnect with several believers in the Duhok area of Kurdistan on November 1, 2008. The last stop was Pastor K's, where we all celebrated together around the same kitchen table where, months earlier, we had literally agonized hour after hour over his shocking imprisonment and uncertain fate. It was a time for great food, stories, laughter, and just rejoicing over all that God had been doing, in spite of (or maybe because of) the many difficulties and tragedies that are so common here. The conversation eventually turned to my dad's ever-deteriorating health and nearly constant state of pain. Everyone always asked about him since they remembered the debilitating stroke he had suffered in the summer of 2005, right in the middle of the Entrust debut season in Kurdistan.

"I am actually getting very excited about Dad meeting his grandson for the first time," I blurted out, surprising even myself.

I could see by the horrified expressions that I needed to explain my obvious delight. So, I told them the whole story of how God's littlest warrior lay dying in the palm of his earthly dad's hand while I was literally screaming on the inside with frenzied rage.

"No, God! How can this be fair? How can you let him die? What a cruel joke! After all we have given up serving you on the mission field...No, no, no!"

All of a sudden, my intense fury and grief were converted into wonderment by the most amazing gift. I am generally not inclined to visions, but it is the only word that fits in this particular instance. It was as if I left my own body and even the hospital room for the briefest of moments, and in that instant, God, in His loving mercy, somehow drenched my senses with an actual glimpse of heaven. The certain reality of what I saw, heard and felt with joy unspeakable permanently cemented the forward focus of my life. I felt strong invisible arms around me and a whisper in my ear: "Him now; you soon, beloved." I knew from that moment on that, as King David announced so long ago, my son would not come back to me, but one day, I would go to him. And what a day of rejoicing that will be!

Thus, to be honest, you should think twice about inviting me to any funerals of believers because, for me, it is definitely a delight-filled reaction. Every time a believer I care about dies, I have a precious repeat whiff of that experience, and I get immensely excited all over again about the absolute reality of eternity and the blessed reunion to come!

As I finished the story that night, I was awestruck. I suddenly re-experienced the memory in an astounding way that was more like a delectable bite than just a whiff. My eyes were abruptly drawn to the clock on the wall. The truth, though I would not know it for another thirteen hours, was that at that exact time, my lifelong, fallible hero, who was also my own dad, was gently called home to glory himself from a hospital bed in Kalispell, Montana.

***

Indeed, there was much discussion in the beginning in Kurdistan about the birth of real hope and God's part in that. Shortly after I arrived, one of the local believers who was associated with the school excitedly showed me a passage in his Arabic Bible that he felt mirrored what was happening here.

"I must show this to everyone I know!" he exclaimed. "People must know there is hope, real hope!" A sentiment echoed perfectly through the elation in the prophet Isaiah's words:

> *The people who walked in darkness have seen*
> *a great light.*
> *For those who lived in a land of deep*
> *shadows—light!*
> *Sunbursts of light!*
> *The boots of all those invading troops, along*
> *with their shirts soaked with innocent blood,*
> *will be piled in a heap and burned, a fire that*
> *will burn for days!*
> *For a child has been born—for us!*
> *The gift of a son—for us!*
> *He'll take over the running of the world.*
> *His name will be Amazing Counselor,*
> *Strong God, Eternal Father, Prince of*
> *Wholeness.*
> *His ruling authority will grow,*
> *and there'll be no limits to the wholeness he*
> *brings.* Isaiah 9:2,5-7(MSG)

Kurdish history is rich, colorful, and surprisingly full of many direct references to the Bible and the activities of the Medes, their chosen ancestors. Thus, certain renditions of stories in the books of Daniel, Ezra and Esther are well-known among the Kurds, and other major prophets such as Isaiah are accepted authorities as well.

A sense of delight was literally palpable here as the general public began to realize that they might have a real future. At that time, it was not uncommon for a group of Kurds to begin dancing in the streets whenever they heard encouragement on the news about Saddam's overthrow. Dance has always been a huge part of their culture, and you will still see it depicted in various art forms. To understand their sense of enormous joy, it is important to remember just how forbidden even the simplest of pleasures were to the Kurds during Saddam's reign and elsewhere in the bigger region. In Turkey, for example, people were often imprisoned for simply uttering the Kurdish language.[11]

I had many memorable conversations during that time with the teachers I was working with about hope and what it means. One shared the following about Newroz, the Kurdish New Year that falls on March 21—the first day of Spring:

"Newroz, this year, is very joyful and special and quite different from the past years. After Operation Iraqi Freedom, all the recently liberated areas which Kurds inhabited are able to celebrate Newroz again together with their friends and families. The Kurds that lived under the rule of Saddam never even uttered the word 'Newroz'. If they did, they would surely have been beheaded."

They offered such tidbits of horror in calm and pragmatic voices. It was simply the way things were for them. If you wanted to stay alive, you tried to remain unseen and in a constant state of identity denial. Many had witnessed the horrific murders of a majority of their family when they were just small children. One minute they would be talking about the weather, and the next, they would casually mention the day the soldiers came to their village and rounded up several families, loading them onto an ancient school bus. Later someone would return to the village with the appalling news that they had seen the bus just before it had been driven into a huge hole and then covered with tons of dirt—burying all of the passengers alive.

The atrocities regularly committed for years by Saddam Hussein and his various henchmen against the Kurdish people leave no doubt in my own mind of just how much a weapon of mass destruction the man himself was against this ethnic group. Hundreds of thousands of Kurdish men, women and children were slaughtered at his decree.

Journalist and author Christiane Bird, who traveled extensively throughout the land in 2003 gathering interviews, reported that even those who fled for their very lives to neighboring Turkey found themselves further persecuted there as refugees:

> "See over there." Siyabend pointed toward a Turkish mountain in the distance, its tip now blue-black, dipped in darkening snow. "That's where we went after the uprising. We stayed in a refugee camp there for two months, and then they sent us to a camp near Mardin. We stayed there four years..."
>
> "Four hundred people died in the first camp," said one of his brothers.
>
> "They tried to poison us with bread in the second," said one of the wives.
>
> "The Turkish soldiers hit the women."
>
> "They kicked the children like footballs."
>
> "But we couldn't come back. Saddam—"
>
> "He gassed his own people."
>
> "He destroyed four thousand Kurdish villages."
>
> "More than one hundred eighty thousand people disappeared."
>
> "How did we survive?"
>
> "God helped us."[12]

Like everything else in Iraq, education under Saddam's regime had been all about him. Every school textbook included various and plentiful references to his might, power, and general greatness. It was a systematic form of intimidation and brainwashing. In the minds of the people, the man became a demon of epic proportions, and they lived in constant terror of his wrath. Further, the only acceptable methodology in the classroom was basic rote memorization. Students were never encouraged to express their creativity or even permitted to learn how to reason or deduce properly. Keeping your mouth shut and repeating after me was the only option.

Imagine then how exciting it was in those early days to see these young adults slowly open up and share what was on their hearts and minds…many for the very first time in their lives. It was much like watching a rare and delicate flower slowly unfold and spread its arms to the sun. You almost wanted to hold your breath, so you did not disturb the phenomenon in progress.

A simple question such as, "What is your favorite color?" would be met with an awkward silence as they pondered and processed such a thought. Then they would look a tad bemused and admit that no one had ever asked them that sort of thing before. Eventually, they would hesitantly begin to describe how happy a certain shade of this or that made them feel when they gazed upon or wore it.

Despite their oppressed history, the people of Kurdistan were delightful—a most intriguing blend of brokenness and humor, intellect and innocence, oppression and resilience, all overlaid with remarkable, childlike optimism and faith that was both humbling and inspiring. Above all, they just wanted to be heard. As an ambassador for Jesus, I knew I needed to be willing to count the full cost of that desire and learn how to embrace the silence, listen well and faithfully affirm.

Concerning their overall spiritual progress, there was, and is, forward movement, to be sure. But even now, it is often in faltering baby steps, which again makes the birthing analogy so apt. Effective mentoring and discipleship are very akin to long-term parenting. There is no shortcut, magic formula or wonder drug. Instead, it is often a matter of simply putting the time in day after day whether you feel like it or not—as Jesus modeled with the disciples. The Word became flesh and dwelt among us that we might personally come to know Truth and be set free by it. It is about being there for the long haul, simply out of love, without detailed agendas or even specific expectations.

Isn't that what God insists successful discipleship in His name is all about? The resemblance to parenting is striking. Well-known author Jerry Jenkins offers the benefits he and his wife discovered while instituting that same kind of time priority policy early on with their own children, despite the challenges and ongoing uncertainties of a writing career:

> Kids—and spouses—hear what you say, but they believe what you do. Maintain your priorities, and your work will benefit.
>
> Every day, I logged between two and three hours with the kids. And we didn't have to be discussing the meaning of the cosmos. Sometimes all they wanted was to climb on me. We played outside. We played inside. We were friends. I was a novelty to the rest of the neighborhood kids because they rarely saw their fathers at all, let alone outdoors.
>
> Other fathers had fallen for the myth of quality time. It went like this: If you spent quality time with your kids, you did not necessarily have to spend a large quantity of time.
>
> But to kids, quality is quantity. The talkative kid wants to talk. The quiet one wants to be quiet. The little one wants attention. Invest the time, and they all get what they need.[13]

The same principles hold true for discipling those who are young in the Lord, particularly if they have had zero societal or generational background in biblical principles and spiritual relationships. Hence, done right, it becomes simple enough, but it is also the most labor-intensive job on the planet.

I am often approached by people who have a desire to serve in a place like Iraqi Kurdistan but are continually thwarted by the notion that they have nothing to offer because they lack formal theological training or specialized skills. What can you do? Just like Jesus, you can be there: to listen, walk alongside, and share in the everyday hardships and dreams, thus earning the right to speak into lives in a meaningful way. Straightforward, no strings attached, quality time works. It always has. Hundreds of well-loved Kurdish proverbs reflect their particular worldview, but they also contain universal truths. One of my favorites is simply this: *"We don't care how much you know until we know how much you care."*

Think about it—no loving parent in their right mind would dream of patting their toddler on the head, handing her or him a copy of life's instruction manual, and simply walking away. For that matter, any onlooker would be completely horrified at the thought of such obvious neglect. As seasoned believers, if we do not follow up short-term evangelism and leadership training with purposeful and ongoing discipleship, isn't that exactly what we become guilty of?

God brought the implications of this particular message home to me in those first years in Kurdistan through watching the growth stages of an actual baby girl in the first years of her life. F and his wife N had been raised Kakai, a Zoroastrian folk religion among many Kurdish tribes based on the teachings of King David. When F heard a simple, straightforward gospel presentation, he realized that there was something missing in his life that he desperately wanted. He began to read the Bible, ask questions, and eventually invited Jesus into his heart and soul. As he, in turn, earnestly shared what was happening inside of himself with his young wife, she too began to inquire about this God who seemed to want to be in some sort of personal relationship.

The couple had been married a few years at the time and had not conceived a child. Sadly, this is a genuinely taboo occurrence in Kurdish culture since having children is automatically equated with ideas of success and prosperity. If the first child is not born within a couple of years, then the extended family will generally even start suggesting that the man needs to consider taking another wife. F did not know it, but N had begun to sincerely talk to this God of his about her deep and ongoing yearning to be pregnant. Shortly after Christmas that year, she learned that her prayers had been answered, and she had conceived. She remains convinced that God Himself heard her prayer and granted her heart's desire out of His abundant love for them. Soon afterward, she too asked Jesus into her heart. Their daughter, M, was born in the fall of 2003, much to the delight of all.

When I first met the six-month-old version of M, I was captivated by both the stories and the baby herself. I even had several opportunities to travel with the family to other cities in Kurdistan for various functions in what was then a world of no day cares, car seats, walkers, or other modern paraphernalia. Hence taking care of the baby became a 24/7 responsibility. It is a matter of all hands on deck, all the time, everyone joyfully pitching in to do their part. It was clear that God expected no less concerning the welfare of the spiritual children that He had so lovingly entrusted to me.

***

Growing up is not particularly easy, either from a physical or spiritual standpoint. It was never meant to be. Jesus steadfastly represented and reinforced this truth all the way to the cross. He did it even in the midst of a shame/honor society where saving face was then, and remains today, always paramount. To be sure, the basic unique tenets of preparing for the coming Kingdom in the way that Jesus portrayed it remains practically unheard of in many places around the world, including one's own neighborhood.

In my mind, to get the job done right anywhere, let alone in a war zone, is still going to take much prayer, lasting commitment, resources of all kinds, and, most importantly, consistent hands-on help of many, many dedicated followers willing to take a turn and carry the baton themselves:

> *Therefore we also, since we are surrounded by so great a cloud of witnesses, let us lay aside every weight, and the sin which so easily ensnares us, and .let us run with endurance the race that is set before us, looking unto Jesus, the author, and finisher of our faith, who for the joy that was set before Him endured the cross, despising the shame and has sat down at the right hand of the throne of God. For consider Him who endured such hostility from sinners against Himself, lest you become weary and discouraged in your souls.*
>
> Hebrews 12:1-3 (NKJV)

Or the same scripture might grab your attention more in contemporary English….whatever works:

> *Do you see what this means—all these pioneers who blazed the way, all these veterans cheering us on? It means we'd better get on with it. Strip down, start running—and never quit! No extra spiritual*

fat, no parasitic sins. Keep your eyes on Jesus, who both began and finished this race we're in. Study how he did it. Because he never lost sight of where he was headed—that exhilarating finish in and with God—he could put up with anything along the way: Cross, shame, whatever. And now he's there, in the place of honor, right alongside God. When you find yourselves flagging in your faith, go over that story again, item by item, that long litany of hostility he plowed through. That will shoot adrenaline into your souls! Hebrews 12:1-3 (MSG)

Chapter Four: What's Your Story?

Making Sense of the Fear

It quickly became apparent as I began to form close relationships with the people of Kurdistan that in order for them to trust me with their own intimate stories, I would need to be honest and transparent with my personal battles. Life stories are an important part of loving one another well, and they forge bonds of trust in ways nothing else can. It takes a bit of work to fashion one's own life story in a manner for others to consume, but it is always well worth the effort.

One of the elements of life in Kurdistan that struck me from the very beginning was the enormous ongoing presence of fear and its devastating power. People were afraid of everything, and with good reason historically. But in 2004, Saddam had been officially toppled, and still, that groundless, paralyzing fear remained, by and large. After all, it was the status quo and was somehow easier. I empathized with that kind of fear and resonated greatly with the enormous hold it still had on every fiber of their beings. Fear is a controlling, intimidating weapon, regardless of whether any actual basis for it can be substantiated. I am fully convinced that it is Satan's favorite tool, and we seldom recognize it.

In truth, I had pondered the effects of fear long before I came to Iraq, as my life's earliest recollections actually began with it.

1962—The little three-year-old girl was terrified but mesmerized by the rage she saw in front of her. She will always remember the feel of the cool, white tile on the wall behind her that she kept pushing against with her tiny balled-up fists, wishing it would somehow provide an unexpected escape. This woman kept acting so strangely; one minute, she was a funny and sweet mommy, yet the next full of fury and despair. This time they were in the kitchen, and the little girl watched as her mother rolled around on the floor screaming and sobbing incoherently. Years later, as the grown-up child retells this story, she realizes that the most poignantly clear piece of this particular memory is that moment in time when the woman makes eye contact with the little girl and says softly with a strange, bright glint in her eyes, "Don't worry, honey; it's just my nerves."

Thus began my own journey with irrational fear, as I was that small child.

Rage is terrifying even when it does not result in direct physical abuse. Unfortunately, some people like my mother are addicted to whatever feelings arise when they unleash verbal wrath. Not only did it radically distort any authentic connection with my mom, but it also, for many years to come, infected every major decision I made in my life, at least in the area of relationships.

School provided a welcome escape, as it felt safe and somehow normal, so I thrived both academically and in extra-curricular activities. I learned early on, however, not to bring friends home since I never knew for sure what would be waiting on the other side of the front door. Decades later, I would hear of the painful emotional voyage that my mother went through as a young woman, complete with multiple hospitalizations and even electric shock treatments. I will always believe that it would have been much better to face the ongoing reality together as a family…but that was not to be.

Even in our world's current zeitgeist, when it seems like almost anything goes, mental illness is sure to label one as a pariah. This can be readily observed around the world. "Be anything you want, just don't be crazy" …as if you have an option. Blood relatives tend to be the most adamant in their denial of its existence in one of their own, probably because of the genetic implications involved. However, pretending things are "normal" when they obviously are not, accomplishes nothing in the end and serves to warp the minds of the innocent children who are involved by default.

Fear demolishes hope and devours trust. In fact, it is telling that even in the West, we do not like to talk about the reality of fear as if it is somehow shameful and only for the cowardly. Yet *"Don't be afraid"* is a constant command throughout scripture, found almost four hundred times throughout both the Old and New Testaments. That kind of emphasis clearly implies both that we will often be tempted to be afraid, and yet, we can and should always choose not to be, with God's help. Interestingly, there is no indication that Jesus ever showed fear, though he displayed almost every other emotion, both negative and positive. In the garden, it was anguish, which is close and yet different. He certainly had countless justified reasons to be afraid at different times during His earthly life, and yet, He never was.

***

Even at the height of Saddam's atrocities, let alone now, Kurdish people seldom share the brutal truth of a situation with their children because they don't want to frighten them. Consequently, they grow up believing there is obviously just something wrong with being Kurdish. As we began to sort out their own life stories, it often started out all sunshine and roses since they had stuffed the horror way down deep in their soul for a very long time. As the truth slowly bubbled to the surface, it was simultaneously heart-wrenching and immensely therapeutic. As my questions continued, they, in turn, asked to know more of my own story.

I was born the second of two children shortly after my parents moved to Seattle, Washington, in 1959. My father, a statistical engineer, chose to pursue a career in Civil Service with the Defense Department, working on the development of the anti-ballistic missile system. This particular program had a fairly mobile headquarters in the interest of security, and we tended to move around for Dad to work at various military bases and government headquarters within the country. Hence, as a family, we relocated about once a year, primarily around the western United States.

In many ways, my childhood was very typical of the carefree life in the suburbs of middle-class America during the 60s and 70s. This period was aptly depicted in the television show *Wonder Years*, which was told from the kid's viewpoint. Even though for me the neighborhoods, and subsequently the friends, changed quite frequently, the overall ambiance was much the same as my own, with the notable additions of church life and mental illness. I was raised within the Presbyterian denomination, just as my mother had been. My father was brought up Catholic and converted to Protestantism upon marriage. Thus, my parents presented a united front on that issue, and we attended both church and Sunday school regularly as a family.

Sadly, my mother's emotional problems caused a special degree of dysfunction within every aspect of the family unit, as a constant priority in life was to do anything and everything to keep Mom from "flying off the handle." As I recall, beyond the occasional bedtime prayers, we never actually discussed salvation or our spiritual lives. In some ways, I think the entire family was under the misguided assumption that enough time in the garage (or church) would somehow make you into an acceptable "car."

As a teenager, I began what could best be termed as a phase of hidden rebellion. My grades and activity involvement remained high, but on the inside, I was rapidly tuning out church and all it stood for. I began to cultivate a group of friends who lived on the wild side, where I was quickly introduced to a number of different vices, most of which I gladly experimented with. After high school graduation, I chose not to go directly to college, mainly because it seemed like everyone in the family expected me to. Instead, I quickly landed a traveling job in the food and beverage industry, where life continued to be one big party for the next couple of years.

On my twentieth birthday, I suddenly realized I would soon be "old" and needed to get serious about a college education. I enrolled at the University of Montana in the fall of 1980 and began a Liberal Arts education. I was required to take a foreign language and chose Classical Greek, as those funny little letters had always fascinated me. Moreover, I knew I would not have to speak it a great deal, and that was important since I had a dreadful experience attempting to speak French in junior high (which would also prove the case with Kurdish in later life). To be sure, Greek quickly became my favorite class. I adored the ideal structure and accuracy of the language and hence was more than willing to commit the time necessary to excel at it.

By the end of the first quarter, we began to carefully translate the Gospel of John, and suddenly the Bible came alive to me in a way that I never dreamed possible. Perhaps this is why I take such delight in Eugene Peterson's *The Message*. A Greek and Hebrew scholar as well as a pastor, it took Peterson ten years to put the Bible into contemporary English. When I compared his version of John's Gospel and my own notes, I was astounded at the similarities. It is remarkable what happens when you take the time to struggle with understanding the original language and then grapple with putting it in one's own words. During this same time, I also had a literature class where we dealt extensively with the Book of Job and the problem of pain, as well as a Humanities class entitled "Introduction to the Judeo/Christian Period," in which we read the works of Dante and St. Augustine.

Suffice to say, despite my attending a very secular, known "party school," I was nevertheless surrounded by the issue of God's place in my life. Then, halfway through that particular quarter, my neighboring dorm mates were all killed in an alcohol-related car crash. Suddenly the whole dorm was vocal about how it was so sad and how fortunate we all were to believe in God and life beyond.

The problem in my mind was that I knew those gals fairly well, and none of us generally acted like we believed in God. At least not the God I was slowly discovering as I translated John's Gospel account word by painstaking word. As I saw it, God would never be content with closet life, only to be pulled out on the occasional human whim. Instead, God expected one's heart and a life-changing commitment in exchange for an adventure in living that seemed quite able to exceed all expectations. I struggled with the inconsistency of it all for several months. I remember hiking in the foothills behind the university and praying intently that if God truly were who He seemed to say He was in His word, then somehow, I needed to meet someone that actually lived that way and was not playing some pseudo-Christianese game. Of course, I was also determined not to "help" God in this endeavor by going to church, or any place else for that matter, that might have easily produced committed believers.

Then spring arrived, and I met a handsome young cowboy who struck up a conversation with me over the word "intrepid." He proceeded to invite me to join him for a cup of coffee. The coffee grew quite cold as he earnestly shared his newfound relationship with Jesus Christ in a simple and direct way. That night on my way home, I pulled over to the side of the road, got out of the car, and on my knees, committed my entire life to the Lord. It was a crossroads, one of those special moments of time that is clearly seared into my memory for life.

Shortly thereafter, I married that cowboy, and over the next two decades, we shared the precious quest of growing up together in the Lord. Now in the interest of brevity, I am going to purposely "lump" a tremendous amount of information within the preceding statement, as it is always so tempting to share the countless little details and Goddities that continually enrich the life of every follower in active pursuit of maturity in Christ. Suffice to say that Bible college, youth ministry, the mission field and an unexpected, miraculous pregnancy all played significant roles in my own journey's tapestry as a married woman.

***

We *all* have a story to share. Thus, we all have a part to play. God, in His infinite love and mercy, designed the whole of creation as a marvelous tale of redemption in which we all get to play a role. His story became history, as they say, and the world will never make sense without intimate knowledge of that foundation and our own part in it. As author John Eldredge points out:

> The story God is telling—like every great story that echoes it—reminds us of three eternal truths it would be good to keep in mind as we take the next step out the door.

First, things are not what they seem.

Where would we be if Eve had recognized the serpent for who he really was? And that carpenter from Nazareth—he is not what he appears to be, either. There is far more going on around us than meets the eye. We live in a world with two halves, one part that we can see and another part that we cannot. We must live as though the unseen world (the rest of reality) is more weighty and more real, and more dangerous than the part of reality we can see.

Second, we are at war.

This is a love story set in the midst of a life-and-death battle. Just look around you. Look at all the casualties strewn across the field. The lost souls, the broken hearts, the captives. We must take this battle seriously.

Third, you have a crucial role to play.

That is the third eternal truth spoken by every great story, and it happens to be the one we most desperately need if we are ever to understand our days. Frodo underestimated who he was, as did Neo, as did Wallace, as did Peter, James, and John. It is a dangerous thing to underestimate your role in the story.

You will lose heart, and you will miss your cues.

This is our most desperate hour. You are needed.[14]

***

The power of one's story simply cannot be denied. Further, Jesus often taught with short stories known as parables. Much discussion has taken place about why Jesus used storytelling extensively, but only over the last fifty years or so has there been a known concerted effort to duplicate His approach. Arguably, the most successful story-oriented evangelical tool developed to date is *The Jesus Film*. It simply brings scripture and the subsequent stories of the Gospel to the screen in the heart language of the listener. It has now been translated into over 1600 languages, shown in every country on the planet, and resulted in over 490 million professions of faith in Jesus as Lord and Savior.[15] What a blessed beginning the film has become to the life-long discipleship process!

As a matter of fact, the whole of the Bible itself is a vast series of stories that can be used in a compelling way to share eternal truth. Much work has been done on this in the last few decades. Just as I arrived in Kurdistan, I was given the opportunity to help with the beginning stages of bringing systematic Bible storying for the first time to the believers of Kurdistan. Help was actively sought and given by The

International Orality Network (ION).[16] Few realize the countless, laborious hours that go into determining what set of Bible stories and subsequent questions are the best to use for a specific ethnic group like the Kurds, with the goal of actually finding Jesus for themselves.

Despite all the hard work of a multitude of committed followers across the wider region, Bible storying has not yet taken off in the Middle East as many hoped it would. Like everything else, it is a slow progression, and the benefit of first-generation believers, in particular, learning the stories of the Bible well enough to explain and share them in digestible morsels is, in fact, priceless beyond measure.

After all, as technological advances continue to increase exponentially around the globe, we have all become oral learners of a sort – taking in nanoseconds of sound bites and information before we move on to the next tidbits – trying diligently to become at least as smart as our own phone. These days, few people have time for any book, let alone one as large, intimidating, and purposefully unclear as the Bible promises to be without the gift of the Holy Spirit (1 Corinthians 2:14).[17]

Jesus also loved people enough to want to hear their stories and continually asked personal questions to which He patiently waited for answers. We know from the interaction with the Samaritan woman[18] that even when He already knew the answer, He still asked because when it comes to relationships, listening matters. Moreover, it is so easy, especially in a place like Kurdistan, to find oneself doing all the talking when it comes to private matters of the heart.

Remember, people here had never been given a chance before to talk about anything personal, let alone their own inner thoughts and who they believe God is. Thus, they do not have ready answers for that type of question, and one needs to embrace silence and develop patience born of love. It is crucial to their own growth, but so, so tempting to just provide them with your own confident, ready-made answers, to which they will smile and nod agreeably as that is the "comfortable" reality that they are used to, especially from the church. The tragedy is that this type of approach simply ends there, without any kind of inner impact on hearts.

Indeed, I have found over the years that given the necessary encouragement and processing time, coupled with the transparency of one's own follies, it slowly becomes fun for national believers to recall the memories, both good and bad, and this eventually results in a time of deep healing and clarity. Further, as they hear the similarities within the stories of the Bible, as well as the personal stories of others in pursuit of God, it opens doors of understanding. In truth, we humans are all made in God's image, and despite huge differences in labels and perspectives, at the end of the day, we can commiserate with everyone's basic struggle to find

God and live life well in the midst of a damaged and crazy world.

***

I am now fully convinced that God looks at earthly suffering completely differently than we expect Him to. I did not learn to practice frequent, earnest listening to and communing with the Lord either until my own life, as I knew it, abruptly imploded. Pain and tragedy, as hard as we try to avoid them, tend to jump-start one's ongoing spiritual journey. Much has been written on this mystery, and God offers the book of Job and the story of Naomi as well as countless examples from nature. Perhaps the most succinct quote I have found comes from the writings of Pastor Peter Marshall when he prayed, "When we long for life without difficulties, remind us that oaks grow strong in contrary winds and diamonds are made under immense pressure."[19]

Pain is part of the deal and has been since the fall. The trouble is that God offers the perfect permanent solution but does not *force us* to listen, and I think we subconsciously expect Him to—the same way that we would in His place. We forget that He designed and fought for our free will from the beginning of time, even when it cost Him greatly. It still comes down to a believer's own choice. He stands at the door and knocks politely—though no one has a greater right than He to barge right in unannounced.

Sadly, we unknowingly think that if God actually wants to talk to us, He is going to hit us over the head with a mighty two-by-four. Maybe, when necessary, He uses our life experiences to clobber us, but rarely when it comes to our individual relationship with Him. Instead, He often reaches out in a loving whisper that, while compelling, is easy to ignore. He does not want submission based on fear, but rather active love based on trust. Think about it—the two cannot coexist. Unfortunately, blind obedience with no choice involved is less scary, especially when your life has always been based on fear. This was true for the children of Israel thousands of years ago, and it is still true today for most of us, especially violently oppressed ethnic groups like the Kurds.

Certainly, the death of my infant son had a profound impact on my life, the greatest of all being the abiding reality of eternity. Johnathan's earthly existence, however brief, settled that question deep within my heart in a way that I am not sure anything else could have.

In the context of my own intimate relationship with God, however, it was the searing agony of a totally unexpected and shockingly ugly divorce after twenty years of marriage that dramatically changed everything for my *eventual* growth. At first, in a state of utter, disbelieving brokenness with a badly tattered heart, I would take long, solitary walks and just cry out to God in anguish. I was a mess. He always answered me through the Holy Spirit, often with an unexpected breeze, a child's smile, or a scripture passage brought to mind. But occasionally, it was more like an undeniable Presence with words clearly heard and felt in my soul.

The turning point arrived one evening when I was tearfully blubbering yet again and suddenly sensed Him almost shake me and say:

My relationship with you is One on one—why do you keep insisting that it has anything to do with anybody else, including your former husband? Never forget that I knew you before you were born, and I will never, ever abandon you to a future without hope.

It was an illuminating moment that I continue to cherish and remember well when times get tough. Okay, Lord, One on one. Considering the Godhead, it's actually Three on one—relationship in absolute perfection inviting you to join. It simply doesn't get better than that.

I feel tremendously sorry for those who do not believe that God directly talks to us—I cannot imagine dealing with daily life without that comforting reality! Jesus is not just a story in a book. God sent His son to earth as a real person so that we can actually be in a relationship…forever. Moreover, the incredible, little-known secret is that the more time you make to give Him, the more He joyfully reveals Himself. That is an unexpected but very real benefit of singleness, which the apostle Paul addresses.[20] Obviously, he is not suggesting that every married person is missing out on a deeper walk. Rather, every human connection, regardless of how seemingly spiritual and deep, must take a back seat to one's own bond with God if life is going to be lived as He intended. There is only one Holy Spirit, and He never gives His job away.

***

It was in that particular post-divorce vein of introspection that I was led to take a women's Bible study authored by an Entrust board member called "Developing a Discerning Heart." God used that course mightily in my life, at that time and since, as I have had the opportunity to lead a few other groups of women through it as well. For perhaps the first time, I examined exactly who I, as an individual, was in Christ. I began to realize just how intent I had been for so long in constructing intricate (but false) wells that I had fervently hoped would satisfy my inner dryness and make life both workable and safe.

In a state of genuine emptiness, I began to examine how I was designed from the beginning for a relationship with God. He has gifted each one of us with the capacities to think, choose, feel, and thirst for true intimacy that can only be found in Him. Confronting my own inherent willfulness and the various cheap imitations I had pursued throughout my life in an erroneous attempt to satiate that internal yearning was a challenging yet beneficial journey. Often it was an excruciatingly painful dive below my own particular waterline, but it was also ornamented with many unexpected moments of joy and growth.

So, it was a new perspective, born out of suffering, that sent me back to the mission field with a deep desire to help others fully discover Him for themselves while recognizing the ongoing folly of fear. Only one exception for the "Do not be afraid" directive exists in the Bible. We are supposed to fear God...just nothing or no one else. I submit that that type of fear is actually more of a motivating devotion that compels us to trust in His perfect love, regardless of the circumstances. The coming months and years demonstrated that I was on the right track.

Chapter Five: Understanding Misunderstandings

Jesus was not an American, and other surprises

American message bearers tend to hit the field enthusiastically with all kinds of ready answers for problems they actually do not have a clue about. I was no different. When you think about it, it's who we are as a nationality. We have been taught for generations that with enough ingenuity and hard work, you can do anything. Many American Christians readily buy into the "God helps those who help themselves" mentality—a popular chant of old in our homeland that is not actually in the Bible or even supported by its truth.

Kurds, on the other hand, were told for decades: "Keep your head down and stay out of sight if you want to survive. Jesus is for others, not for you; you are Kurdish after all."

Why then is there such a unique affinity between these two people groups? Perhaps it is a case of "opposites attract." Or it could be the long-buried hope that one day, the people of Kurdistan, too, will be recognized as an independent nation, serving the world in their own right. No matter, in my early years of living among them, the men of Kurdistan were always most eager to meet Americans in particular, swap tales, and share several cups of tea together.

There is an old Scottish poem written by Robert Burns in the 1700s entitled *"To the Louse."* It is a story about a woman with a louse (small insect = singular of lice) in her bonnet that others see, but the woman herself does not know about. Thus, as she thinks everyone is pointing out her incredible beauty and wonderful hat, she begins to smile and preen accordingly. The most famous line of the poem is at the end, where the poet laments that we could save ourselves a lot of embarrassment if God would give us the gift to actually see ourselves as others see us.[21]

Without any hesitation, I submit that it would be greatly beneficial if every American traveling abroad were presented with that same gift. It would be a wonderful blessing for those of us who live cross-culturally and are constantly put in the position of having to explain the clueless behavior of our beloved country folk. Certainly, it is not everybody, but unfortunately, a few obnoxious and inappropriate idiots have given many non-Americans a sour taste for the people of the United States and, frankly, rightly so—spend a little time people-watching in a foreign airport, and you are sure to be embarrassed too. As Americans, we have tremendous strengths but also significant weaknesses. Moreover, it is universally common to lump people together by nationalities along with whatever is happening on the world stage politically at any given moment. Ordinary

Americans overseas can go from the greatest heroes to the most despicable villains, all in the blink of an eye.

Further, within the mission world, there has been a significant shift in the last decade regarding who the active majority church actually is these days. America used to lead the charge in mission endeavors all over the globe, but that is no longer true, and we either have to adapt or become irrelevant. Paul Borthwick addresses this issue in depth in his book *Western Christians In Global Mission: What's the Role of the North American Church?* Perhaps most telling were the three questions that the majority of the World's church leaders from Africa and Asia asked at a global Lausanne movement conference:

1. Does the church in America have a prophetic role in its own society or does it simply mimic the culture and entertain its members?

2. Does the church in America have the humility to learn from us or do they consider themselves to be the world's teacher?

3. Does the American church have the magnanimous spirit to work alongside us in a genuine partnership that is based upon mutual respect and shared resources, or do

they simply see us as their "partners" to fulfill their plans in our countries?[22]

To be fair, as always, there is another side to this story. But you might be surprised and dismayed to hear honest answers to such questions from U.S. pastors and ministry leaders these days. We may not ever verbalize it, but our actions and our pocketbooks speak volumes about our actual priorities.

To be sure, we as Americans were in the minority of message bearers when I arrived in Iraqi Kurdistan. Most of the faith workers were Europeans, Australians, and South Americans, who had been faithfully tilling the hard soil for years. They were somewhat leery of Americans in general since Operation Iraqi Freedom had recently commenced and opinions, though seldom voiced, were clearly negative.

Without question, war is a horrific, devastating reality, but it has existed since the beginning of time and shows no signs of disappearing. Further, scripture makes it clear that at the end of the day, it all remains under God's control, regardless of what the politicians advocate for or against. All I really know is what I experienced. God has one single endgame, and that is rescuing souls. The conflict for a chance at freedom opened massive doors within people's hearts, and that alone must be celebrated rather than cursed.

It is the unheard legacy of every single service person that shed blood on Iraqi soil.

Native ethnic groups in the developing world tend to lump all expatriate (foreign) workers into the same pile, which is always awkward. In reality, there are significant and growing cultural and worldview differences among, and even within, the various "first-world" societies, let alone when you add others. In Kurdistan, though, there was a glaring exception that actually made it worse. Kurdish people tended instead to lump foreigners into two groups—there were the AMERICANS, and then there were the other internationals. It made proper networking a huge challenge. The Kurds, at that point, were completely enraptured with the notion of the United States at the expense of all other nationalities. Unfortunately, they would openly share that fact with anyone who would listen. N & G, a beloved, seasoned Bulgarian couple that had served with Entrust for many years, experienced this peculiar brand of racism in Kurdistan, and I will never forget the enduring lessons of grace and love they taught me by example.

The truth was that the Kurds did not actually know individual Americans, but they idolized the concepts of freedom, power, and the inalienable right to pursue life, liberty, and happiness as each saw fit. They emulated the wealth, arrogance, and confidence they saw in the USA as constantly represented on the news. Remember, Kurdistan was always safe and peaceful during Operation Iraqi Freedom, so they did not interact much at all with real live combat soldiers. It was more about the dream they perceived us to represent than the reality of an authentic relationship. For many, especially in the rural areas, I was the first genuine American, let alone Christian, that they had ever actually met.

A film released in 2012 entitled *"BEKAS"* shares the same fascination and hero-worshiping devotion so often found among Kurds for the USA. It is a well-written script about two young, homeless Kurdish brothers in Iraqi Kurdistan who live on the edge of survival in the difficult times of the early 90s. At the beginning of the story, they catch a glimpse of Superman through a hole in the wall at the local cinema. The boys decide that they want to go to America and live with Superman.[23]

This type of adoring sentiment was still going strong in the early 2000s. Many Kurds even repeatedly expressed a desire for Kurdistan to become the 51st state. Over the years, the subject still comes up regularly among the older generation whenever the tea shop discussion turns to a long-term solution. "We are not Arabs, or Persians, or Turks, and yet, as Kurds, we don't trust each other or work together well enough to stand on our own against the enemies that abound. We need to be part of something bigger and stronger that will allow us to live in peace and freedom, regardless of our politics or religion."[24]

The strong familial affinity cross-culturally also created huge chasms of unexpected misunderstandings and a trail of broken promises that were often not even knowingly made, much less intentionally fractured. Americans tend to speak "dream lingo." We like to think in terms of opportunities and prospects. We talk about what could happen, and we are always abundantly free with sure-sounding advice about almost anything. The Kurds hear it differently. They actually hear promises rather than possibilities and solid backup action rather than theoretical encouragement.

The reality of this conundrum became much clearer when I moved out to the Iran border region of Iraqi Kurdistan in 2013. I relocated to a district known as Raparin, which means uprising or revolution, depending on who you ask. It actually was given its name because of the events that happened in this area on March 5, 1991. This was the time of Desert Storm, and President George H.W. Bush made a public plea that February to the Iraqi people to overthrow Saddam Hussein and reclaim their country:

> "But there's another way for the
> bloodshed to stop, and that is for the Iraqi
> military and the Iraqi people to take matters
> into their own hands, to force Saddam

Hussein, the dictator, to step aside and to
comply with the United Nations resolutions,
and then rejoin the family of peace-loving
nations."[25]

What the ordinary Kurd heard from that speech was that one of the most powerful men on Earth at the time, the President of America, where Superman lives, was asking for their help in overthrowing an evil tyrant that was ruining their very lives and needed to be stopped. Surely if they answered his plea, America would consider them part of the 'family' and would come to the rescue and make sure they were victorious. So, on that long-ago day in early March, it was actually not the military or various politicians that rose up—at least not in the beginning. Instead, it was the ordinary country folk of the Raparin area who bravely left their shops and farms to revolt against a madman intent on genocide.

In the end, no one from the outside helped the Kurdish people, and they were slaughtered by the thousands and began to flee on foot across the snowy mountains into Iran to escape a vengeful, certain death. Many died on the way and were buried where they fell. Eventually, though, the international news of this huge and tragic exodus gave way to the formation of the no-fly zone and the semi-autonomous region of Kurdistan within Iraq. So, in one sense, Raparin is the Kurdish Alamo.

Surely this was a memorable first step toward recognition from the outside world, but for the most part, the Kurdish people still remained completely cowed. Saddam persisted larger than life in most minds, and their terror knew no bounds. Most were immobilized by the nebulous "what-if" dread and horrified by the occasional rumor that the killing would begin again at any moment. Besides, there was no sense of wider community among the Kurdish people. For years, they had not even been allowed to travel from one city in the Kurdish area to another without obtaining an expensive and difficult visa. Divide and conquer was the regime's standard mode of operation. Making a difficult situation even worse, Saddam built ring roads around the larger Kurdish cities and patrolled them relentlessly in hopes of capturing escaping Peshmerga guerrilla fighters trying to get to the safety of the rugged mountains.

I have heard well-meaning, believing American colleagues lament that Desert Storm protected the Kurds and there was no need for Operation Iraqi Freedom. From the perspective of one who lived there, I vehemently disagree. In fact, when the U.S. administration changed in 2008, many Americans meeting people from Iraqi Kurdistan for the first time would try to apologize for the disaster of the war. My Kurdish friends were always greatly troubled by this and would tirelessly correct anyone who tried to call Operation Iraqi Freedom an invasion of any kind. For them, it will always serve as a liberation. However, it was not until Saddam was actually toppled and removed from power that the Kurds began to tentatively dream that maybe, just maybe, a homeland of their own might be a possibility sometime in the distant future.

***

Religious doctrine is another source of constant confusion, as most believe they understand the basic tenets of the "other side" when, in fact, they are often completely wrong. Muslims are generally taught a bit about Jesus. They accept the virgin birth, miracles performed, and his prophetic status to a point. In short, He is presented as a kind of deputy persona to Mohammed, the founder of Islam. They also believe that the Bible has been totally corrupted and cannot be trusted at all. Muslim children have heard these things in school since kindergarten. While they have theoretical respect for Jesus as a prophet, they fear Christians and react accordingly. What a surprise.

Moreover, in a well-meaning but misguided contest to build the church, first-generation believers are quickly forced into positions of authority without any solid foundation or prayerful preparation for the inevitable battle ahead. Sadly, often their own theology becomes a twisted mix of Bible and Koran verses along with a great deal of cultural folk traditions and politics. I was immensely troubled to realize years later that, despite the excellent theological training that Entrust offered over a five-year period, our Muslim-background believing leaders, for the most part, never caught on to either the absolute reality of eternity or the ongoing daily certainty of vicious, spiritual warfare. As you can imagine, such crucial gaps left them vulnerable and open to a variety of brutal attacks, especially from within.

The sad fact is that often people from a variety of religious backgrounds desire to be leaders for the wrong reasons, especially in a deeply oppressed area where brute power is supreme, and money changes everything. In short, the individuals who immediately come to the forefront with hands raised to be part of any management type program are often the last ones that God would choose. Just take a journey through scripture and look at the Lord's various selections for shepherds of His people. Over and over again, throughout the Old and New Testaments, we see bizarre examples that befuddle our tiny minds and leave us scratching our heads in confusion. Just because we do not understand God's choices does not make them any less His perfect selection.

In the end, even in the church, although we have been clearly warned not to lean on our own understanding, we often revert to man's style. Nowadays, this approach is often seen in high-powered corporate thinking, where efficiency and output are all important. God's opinion is seldom asked for, at least with any expectation of an actual answer. In this high-tech, ever-changing world, where we are quite full of ourselves and our own knowledge and accomplishments, we sometimes forget that, in God's eyes, all that we can ever know on this side of heaven is still absolutely minuscule compared to what there *is* to know of Him and His universe.

The trouble is time, or lack thereof, that strange little finite force that never leaves our earthly consciousness and never enters His eternal thoughts:

"Beloved, be not ignorant of this one thing: that with the Lord one day is as a thousand years, and a thousand years as one day." 2 Peter 3:8 (NKJV)

We read it, we memorize it, but we do not believe it in our human core. Subsequently, in our own constant rush, we do not take the time needed to listen well to those we come to serve or even to God Himself. After all, the mantra is incessant: *Time is short, the harvest is at hand; we have the gospel to share with the nations —"by golly, let's get a move on!"*

Undeniably, all kinds of language difficulties and comprehension issues are a huge source of ongoing misunderstandings as well. Furthermore, even when they are not the problem, in reality, they will almost always get the blame, as it is an easy fallback that everyone accepts.

You may be familiar with economist Alan Greenspan, who said:

> I know you think you understand what you thought I said, but I'm not sure you realize that what you heard is not what I meant....I guess I should warn you, if I turn out to be particularly clear, you've probably misunderstood what I've said.[26]

Such was established to remind people of comprehension problems even when you share the same general culture and heart language, a term which refers to the first language one learned to speak as a small child. I am sure you can imagine how understanding difficulties increase dramatically when you are dealing with multiple heart languages and worldviews all different from your own. From the beginning, the Entrust program in Kurdistan worked with both Arabic and Kurdish speakers through translation in four separate small groups.

We also made several fairly successful attempts to bring all the groups together (triple-translated) in a relaxed retreat or camp mode where having fun and worshiping collectively were the main objectives. It was a delicate process that also included a healthy dose of international resident message bearers and their children who needed the rest and play just as much as the national believers. Further, the resident expats provided cultural understanding and a needed buffer between the multiple ethnicities as well as informal translation for the visiting work team. Servant-hearted teammates and friends from the USA delivered a little teaching, childcare, youth workers and lots of plain ole fun. It began to build a sense of God's larger community among all of us at that time and was uniquely popular in the beginning. I dubbed it family camp as I had had wonderful experiences at such events in various churches back in the States.

Almost immediately, though, I realized we had a problem with the word "family." In short, regardless of your testimony or age in the Lord, you are not considered a true part of God's family in Kurdistan unless you are married. Further, if you are married but your spouse is not a believer, the church tends to view you differently as well. Single men in Iraq are mistrusted by the organized church and get extraordinarily little respect in society. In short, they are just one step above women. Add a conversion experience into the mix, and a single person faces loneliness and ostracization in all directions. As usual, God's innate sense of humor was clear to me in terms of the general state of affairs. You see, in our groups, most of the single Kurdish believers were male and constantly asking us to find them believing wives, whereas most of the single Christian-background Arabs were female, hoping to find a Protestant husband.

Unfortunately, both sides were adamant against mixed marriages, and their only reasoning was that their cultures would never accept that sort of union, regardless of sharing the same faith. This has not changed in all the years I have lived here. In the rare instances where a Kurdish person marries a non-Kurdish person, it is usually a western international rather than an Arab. The depth and power of the angst that still exists between the two ethnicities is obvious in every facet of life in Iraq. Those who have extensively studied the history, like Stephen Mansfield, are perplexed and dismayed, therefore, when they realize that all sides of the world political arena continually chant the same worn-out fallacy:

> There were many errors. Among the worst of them has been that since the nation of Iraq sprang fully formed from European imaginations in the early 1920s, the world has expected the Kurds to be Iraqis. It does not seem to matter that the Kurds were already an ancient people centuries before Rome was an empire. It does not seem to matter that the world once promised the Kurds a Homeland of their own. It does not seem to matter that an Iraqi regime has warred against the Kurds almost from the

moment Iraq became a nation. None of this deterred the nations of the world from insisting the Kurds be good Iraqis and live obediently under a regime that despises them.[27]

It is rare to find native Arabic speakers residing in Kurdistan who are making any effort to learn Kurdish. Autonomous region or not, they basically feel that it's beneath them—after all, it is still Iraq, an Arabic nation. There is definitely ongoing racial tension between the two groups, and to most Middle Eastern minds, the Kurds remain interloping hillbillies that will never have the wherewithal to govern themselves properly. There is also a strong ulterior motive for this thinking, considering the resource-rich land that the Kurds currently occupy in four separate nations. Moreover, the Kurdish language is separated into a number of dialects that further divide the people from themselves.

For the sake of building relationships, though, no matter what, it is important to at least try when it comes to language learning. Like me, you may not actually master it, but that never seems to matter as much as the effort itself. Naturally, Kurds are thrilled when visitors honestly attempt to learn Kurdish, and officials are becoming more determined that citizens and resident card holders must at least have the basics. I am thankful to say that I have passed the informal version of this new requirement at multiple checkpoints nowadays. But without any doubt, smiles, laughter, and ongoing friendships play a huge part in the process.

Personally, conquering Kurdish has been a constant struggle as both tone deafness and now age work against me mightily. Additionally, though I love interactive teaching, I have never been much of a social talker. I am basically an introvert who feels most comfortable hanging out inside my own head. Certainly, I relish a serious heart-to-heart, but daily chatting with a strong cultural tendency to head straight into gossiping drains my spirit in a big way. Most Kurdish acquaintances now tell me my Kurdish is good, meaning barely passable. The problem is, in this society, a passing grade is 50 percent or above. In short, this means I have accomplished a solid D-, at least on a good day. So, to be honest, I live in a fairly constant state of humiliation in this area which sends me to my knees on a regular basis. God's loving answer is always the same:

"Trust Me, my strength is made perfect in your weakness."
2 Corinthians 12:9 (NIV)

It's true. Despite my own mortification over my language shortcomings, many times in rural Kurdistan, I have actually seen my elite status as a native English speaker, coupled with my lack of true fluency in Kurdish, build bridges of safety for Kurdish English learners. These dear folks have many questions about Jesus and Christianity and feel quite comfortable talking to me about them in English—confident that even if I wanted to, I would not be capable of "telling" on them. After all, a vast majority of the older, wider Raparin community does not understand English and does not really want to at this point in time. Even more troubling, the younger generation does not know Arabic very well at all, which is frightening when you consider their geographic location and the brewing troubles in the wider region. Still, by and large, the Kurdish millennials continue to claim English as their second language, largely ignoring Arabic altogether.

To be fair, it is certainly not impossible for non-Kurds to become fluent in Sorani Kurdish; there are some fine examples of triumph among the message bearers scattered throughout Kurdistan. Unfortunately, though, there are countless more examples of defeat and eventual departure as it does get incredibly old—no one likes to be constantly chastised and always incorrect…even when it is good for you. Agenda-oriented workers often resort to continuous translation, and for obvious reasons, this was the Entrust standard procedure for classes. Unfortunately, that brings a third party's opinion into play, which causes other serious problems of its own.

The main trouble is multiple dialects and a lack of standards within each one. Sorani is the chosen official dialect of Iraqi Kurdistan, so children even in Behdini-speaking areas are taught Sorani in school. Sounds straightforward enough until you actually attempt to learn Sorani. Each community handles "the basics" a bit differently in terms of sounds and word choices. Thus, if you move around at all within Kurdistan, you are constantly corrected on phrases your last tutor taught you, and you had been faithfully practicing ad nauseum, only to find out you are wrong, at least in the eyes and ears of your newest tutor. Know also that the love of debate on any topic, including language, is a significant part of the modern Kurdish mindset.

Let me give you an example. I get invited out to eat in homes quite often, so I wanted to know what was best to say after "thank you" when people immediately beckon you inside their home with a big smile and a hearty Kurdish "Welcome." My two staff at the time, who were from separate small communities in the Raparin district, immediately disagreed on what would be proper to say. One taught me to say the equivalent of "I am very happy to be here." The other was adamant that I actually should say the equivalent of "It's nice for me to be here." So...? Like I said, they love to argue, even when there is not a lot to base it on, or it's a relatively minor matter. Furthermore, as a culture, they tend to be circular learners: a belief that the answer will come when everyone is included, and a diverse array of thoughts are considered. It subjectively seeks to find what is meaningful and allow that understanding to infuse everything we do.[28]

So, in the case of the above example, the next step in the process was to ask for others' opinions, their parents in particular. Only after that had been done did they come back to me together and say that it was probably okay for me to use either one…

Even when you are dealing with simple words, the chances for grave misunderstandings are prevalent, due in large part to the differing worldviews. Take the word "no." In the west, teaching your young child that no means no is a fairly standard *modus operandi* for parenting. That is not true in Kurdistan. I was sharing this particular concept with a young Kurdish mother while we watched her two-year-old act out like a terrorizing mini-monster while wholly ignoring his mother's frantic pleas to cease. Her reply was telling.

She explained that there were two problems with what I was saying. One is that Kurdish people generally do not believe that young children should be disciplined much at all, as it can quench their tender spirits, and they are truly innocent at this age. Further, in Kurdistan, among family, "no" does not actually mean "no." Instead, "no" means basically that you disagree, and you do not think your child or your sibling or whoever should do whatever foolishness they're thinking of or planning to do. But in the end, you love them, and thus you will not forbid them, regardless of the inherent danger. They are free now, like all Kurds are free, to make their own choices, good or bad.[29]

This same notion came up repeatedly in a personal and painful way during the war with ISIS as I watched dozens of young people, many college graduates that I had taught, take off for places unknown, often by foot. They continued to leave—even after people started regularly drowning in the desperate sea-crossing attempts or were imprisoned in Turkey. Furthermore, most began this difficult new life by lying about their citizenship, claiming to be Iranian Kurds who had lost their papers, hoping to ensure asylum. It was quite obvious and widely acknowledged, from all that we were seeing and hearing, that one of the safest places to be during the ongoing battle was *inside* Kurdistan—still, they left, over and over again, partly from invasive hopelessness and partly from groupthink.[30] Yet no one really tried to stop them. Again, when you love someone, no does not mean no in Kurdistan.

This also explains the ill-fated referendum for independence in 2017. Even though all the major governments other than Israel were vocal in their disapproval of the obvious politically charged timing, the Kurds felt that they were merely voicing their legitimate desire for eventual self-rule. Again, in their thinking, no does not really mean no, and the world must somehow be grateful for all that the Kurdish military had done to stop ISIS.

From my own perspective, the four years of the ISIS advance into Iraq (2014-2018) were the hardest of all as I literally watched their newfound hopes begin to wilt and die right along with their brave soldiers. It was actually a year before this conflict started, in 2013, that I had moved out to Raparin, the rural district on the Iraq-Iran border. My new community was made up of a large percentage of military families. Thus, as the ruthless slaughter began, I grieved alongside many Peshmerga relatives who had, yet again, lost loved ones in what appeared to be the most bizarre conflict ever, with America seemingly playing both sides in a rather noticeable manner. The Kurdish region remained in this amazing bubble of hospitality and peace through it all, but the people began to feel abandoned, and besides hurting mentally, they were deeply shaken spiritually by the various ISIS atrocities committed in the name of their beloved Islam.

For two and a half years, the Kurdish military held off ISIS with almost no help. Over 1700 Peshmerga died while nearly 10,000 were brutally wounded. Pictures of the fallen lined the streets in every community. Meanwhile, the region was flooded with close to 2 million traumatized refugees, and the problems just kept coming. Further, ordinary citizens took the brunt of it all, as the Kurdish government literally went broke and turned on itself. Party politics became so polarized that crazy and stupid things happened, and a general stalemate between provinces started to occur that continues to some extent even now. As far as the people were concerned, trust in either the Erbil or Baghdad government was at an all-time low.

Hence, when the independence survey vote was called for, I fully expected to see low numbers and the vote itself to be remarkably close or even fail. Yet, when that day actually dawned, suddenly, the indomitable spirit that truly defines Kurdistan rose up once again and whole families, dressed in traditional clothes, walked hand in hand to the polls. The air was festive and full of expectation, with an exceptionally high voter turnout of 89% and over 92% in favor of working toward independence.

Of course, Baghdad's retribution for simply casting a vote was swift and decisive overkill, with the willing and eager help of the Iran regime. Once again, it was time to put those uppity Kurds in their place…In fact, focused efforts were made for a time after the vote to get all international and particularly American civilians kicked out of the country for being illegal since we have never needed or been able to obtain an Iraqi visa in the Kurdistan region. Meanwhile, believing Iraqis left in droves as the evil spirit of fear descended and engulfed the minds and hearts of otherwise rational beings. Moreover, as Baghdad steadily aligned more closely with Tehran, there was also a definite sense of growing apprehension on their side concerning the ongoing, uncanny closeness between Americans and Kurds.

And rightly so, since when you hear the dreams and stories of the Kurds, they resonate strongly with the "American DNA." They just want to be free to live quietly in peace as Kurdish people who are allowed to choose their own religion and raise their families in safety as they see fit. That was the hope they felt the American soldiers brought, and the individual soldiers I had the honor of meeting gave the same reasons as to why they had come. Politics muddies the water continually, but "liberty and justice for all" is still a foundational refrain in the hearts of our brave service people who believe it deeply enough to risk everything.

***

Another common source of disputes is widely different perceptions about the way the world works and our particular role in it. This is the concept commonly known as a worldview, and it is critically important to examine one's own more closely as well as that of your intended ministry target. Thus, one of the first preparatory tasks I was given before I ever came to Iraq was to become familiar with the religion of Islam. Since 9-11, there had been a great deal of suspicion and fear about Islam in general and Muslims in particular.

Consequently, it was an obvious answer to prayer that I was immediately steered toward a seminar hosted by the Navigators[31] and led by one of their long-time staff, Dr. Nabeel Jabbour. Nabeel is an author, lecturer, and expert on Muslim culture. Jabbour's background includes two perspectives—that of the Arab/Muslim world and that of the western/Christian world. He frequently speaks at churches and teaches at seminaries, interpreting the phenomenon of Islamic fundamentalism and other Middle Eastern issues to Westerners and especially Christians.

Originally from Lebanon, Dr. Jabbour lived fifteen years in Egypt and then moved to the USA in 1991. He does understand cross-cultural challenges better than most. He was born into a Christian family but grew up surrounded by Muslims and their culture. I will never forget my first actual conversation with him. In introducing myself, I made some inane comments about why I wanted to go to Iraq and reach out in love to Muslims and persecuted believers alike. His voice was quiet and unassuming as he responded, "Oh, and how many Muslims do you know?"

To this day, I can recall the intensity of the gaze he gave me as he waited tolerantly for my response. I literally felt pinned to the proverbial wall as I looked at him, and I could not help but wonder if this was the same compelling manner Jesus used so often in informal discourses with an individual. The answer, of course, was that I did not know any at that time, and I am quite sure that Nabeel already suspected that when he asked the question.

Moreover, most of the information on Islam that I had been taught up to that point came from well-meaning American Christian "experts" who knew a lot of biased, often hate-filled theories but didn't know any individuals either. It was a telling moment, and the seminar itself went on to challenge a multitude of preconceived notions – many of which I did not even know I held. While I do not personally agree with all that he presents, I will always be thankful that he made me wrestle with these ideas before I was ever launched into Kurdistan.

One of his offerings that had a powerful impact on me at that time was realizing that my own primarily American evangelical tool kit was woefully inadequate. It lacked relevance to the general worldview of Muslims. Nabeel had created a character named Ahmad, a representative composite of several young Muslim men he had had the opportunity to befriend as they attended university in the USA. Ahmad has this to say about the various conversion attempts he was subjected to:

> You see things and explain them with
> legal terminology as if we are in a court. You
> talk so much about guilt and righteousness,
> sin and its penalty, condemnation and
> justification. I've been shown the "Four

Spiritual Laws," the "Bridge to Life" illustration and "Steps to Peace with God." They all follow logical syllogism and use legal terminology. My paradigm or lens through which I look at reality is not primarily that of guilt and righteousness like yours, but that of shame and honor, clean and unclean, fear and power. When I talk with you, it feels like you are laying a guilt trip on me. Does your message have anything to say to me about my shame, my defilement and my fear?"

The character then goes on to offer what could be termed an offensive riddle at first glance...

"When you do what you call "witnessing" to us, you assume that you understand our religion. You start with wrong assumptions by comparing our Prophet Mohammed to Christ and comparing the Qur'an to the Bible. You think that you have us figured out and understand our theology. I am sorry to say you have a skewed understanding of our religion. A true understanding of Islam necessitates that you compare Christ, the way you understand him, to the Qur'an, the way we understand it. You believe that Christ is the eternal, uncreated Word of God, and we believe that the Qur'an, and not Mohammed, is the eternal, uncreated Word of God. The way you think of Christ is the way we think of the Qur'an. So who is equally as important in your religion as the Prophet Mohammed is in ours? And what would your Bible compare to in our religion? Unless you solve this Riddle, you will never understand our theology."[32]

The problem with growing up in an influential, first-world society like America is one tends to unconsciously assume that our own theological viewpoint and worldview are the center of universal Truth, and that is a lie. To wrestle in prayer with Ahmed's riddle seems almost heretical until God begins to reveal surprising answers that were there all along.

So often in mainstream American evangelical circles, we try to put Jesus in a (faulty) box that makes sense to us—instead of consciously using His actions to guide our own understanding, even when following such a unique standard becomes painful and lonely. The resurgence in the 90s of the phrase "What Would Jesus Do?" (WWJD) attempted to bring back this filter to a believer's mind concerning handling daily life. Almost immediately, the idea came under "righteous" fire as being irreverent and problematic in many theological circles. However, when I started to look at it as daily guidance rather than a catchy slogan and diligently searched scripture for answers, it began to dramatically change my own thinking.

The unorthodox and often surprising actions of Jesus throughout the gospels simply do not fit our American Christian model very well. I began to ask God often to reveal my missteps as only He can. This led to ample study of the gospel stories in multiple versions and Jesus' own actions and reactions in every situation. He regularly offers the most disturbing, unexpected statements of Truth. Moreover, they are usually pointed directly at us, His kids, rather than the infernal "bad guys"...

A Simple Guide for Behavior

Don't pick on people, jump on their failures, criticize their faults—unless, of course, you want the same treatment. That critical spirit has a way of boomeranging. It's easy to see a smudge on your neighbor's face and be oblivious to the ugly sneer on your own. Do you have the nerve to say, "Let me wash your face for you," when your own face is distorted by contempt. It's this whole traveling road-show mentality all over again, playing a holier-than-thou part instead of just living your part. Wipe that ugly sneer off your own face, and you might be fit to offer a washcloth to your neighbor.

Don't bargain with God. Be direct. Ask for what you need. This isn't a cat-and-mouse, hide-and-seek game we're in. If your child asks for bread, do you trick him with sawdust? If he asks for fish, do you scare him with a live snake on his plate? As bad as you are, you wouldn't think of such a thing. You're at least decent to your own children. So don't you think the God who conceived you in love will be even better?

Here is a simple, rule-of-thumb guide for behavior: Ask yourself what you want people to do for you, then grab the initiative and do it for them. Add up God's Law and Prophets, and this is what you get.

Matthew 7:1-12 (MSG)

I was often surprised and ashamed of all that I had missed before. The more I prayed, the more He answered. Gradually I began to understand all that I had initially misunderstood about God's mission, spiritual life formation, and the American way.

106

Chapter Six: I Am Woman

What to do when you are just *a girl*

The overhead light was blinding, and I rolled over with a groan, unwilling to immediately leave the warm cocoon of deep sleep. Funny how bright light in the middle of the night is just as insistent for a response as the shrillest alarm clock ringing. What time was it anyway? Bleary eyes sought to focus on the small travel clock beside me on the floor. 2:53 blinked back at me. Considering the darkness outside, that would definitely be AM—ah, the joys of life in Kurdistan.

It was 2007, and general full-power electricity still remained in extremely short supply, averaging between 2-3 hours in a twenty-four-hour period. As to an expected schedule, I am sure that someone, somewhere, probably knew, but they certainly were not telling the rest of us.

If only I could remember to turn off light switches when I blew out the candles each night, I would not keep having these rude awakenings. Of course, that would also mean I would miss this special window of opportunity. Despite the strange hour, I knew that I could, and should, choose to take full advantage of this. I needed to wash a load of clothes, vacuum, print out those waiting documents, and maybe even curl my hair. Now fully awake, I heard my landlord and family making the same types of choices in the house above.

Electricity is a funny thing, so easy to take for granted until you do not have it very often.

I slowly sat up with a sigh and pulled the covers around me to ward off the constant chill of winter, thinking again of how blessed I was to have found this little one-bedroom flat tucked away in a quiet Kurdish neighborhood beneath a local family's new house. To the eyes of the ever curious, it appears that I am simply a border, which, admittedly, would have been the most culturally appropriate scenario for a single woman—especially in those days. In reality, two completely separate residences existed behind the locked gate of a shared carport. It allowed me just a tad of independence and quiet space where I could recharge and freely share all that I was feeling with the Lord. To the uninformed, it might even have seemed as if I liked talking to myself, but at least He and I knew better.

As I awkwardly got to my feet from the thin mattress on the floor and started the tasks at hand, my mind wandered back to the Bible study on Genesis that I had attended the night before. I was still bothered by that unexpected look at women and control issues. Lord, just how much of Eve's motivation to sin came from a desire to be in charge, or at the very least, completely in the know?

Being female has its challenges, but I am very thankful for the uniquely special "wiring," though I do realize that it is often that extra dose of relational sensitivity and heightened curiosity that gets females in the most trouble. I have met with small groups of single expatriate women serving in the region who gather together to pray, encourage one another, and share stories. It was enlightening to all of us to acknowledge how often these particular themes of control and lesser status appear and result in unfortunate and sometimes dangerous choices.

***

"Public announcement #1: I am not God; Public announcement #2: neither are you." I first heard that in a sermon in the early 80s in a little country church in Utah. The foundational element of it has been a comfort of grand proportions for me as a single female on this rocky road of ministry. After all, scripture clearly explains that, while we are made in His image, we neither think nor act like God…any of us, regardless of gender.[33]

Further, the boundless extent of His love for an individual soul makes it clear that neither sex, ethnicity, nor station in life is a determinate of the depth of our own personal relationship with God. The apostle Paul stresses this truth in Galatians 3:28:

There is neither Jew nor Greek; there is neither slave nor free man, there is neither male nor female; for you are all one in Christ Jesus.

I also feel blessed to have grown up in a society that at least considers the whole matter a worthy issue of deliberation. Still, a clear delineation exists throughout scripture regarding inherent differences between males and females. It is quite confusing. I have sat through several excellent debates amongst the hierarchical and egalitarian camps in the realm of Christian ministry.[34] Both sides have many superb scripturally based arguments…which is probably why you seldom see anyone actually *change* positions.

A certain order exists that cannot be denied. The male was created first and then the woman, specifically as a helpmate and comforter. Each had equally important but different roles in creation. I have spent much time in the last decade prayerfully studying Jesus' earthly ministry as the obvious perfect model for discipleship—I find He never does anything without intention. The fact that Jesus did not formally call a female apostle in the choosing of the original twelve has always been revealing for me. He certainly could have, as he was quick to break cultural norms in his dealings with women when it was important for the individual, such as the exchange with the Samaritan woman at the well. Behind the scenes, beloved women were with Him throughout his ministry and travels and evidently served as learners, hosts, financial helpmates and emotional comforters.[35] His incredible love for the individual women in His life then and now is also continually apparent, yet He still chose to draw this initial line in the organizational sand.

It is simply one of those mysteries that we will understand…one fine day when we no longer care.

Moreover, who do you think is actually behind that incessant desire within the female psyche in particular to be in command and able to figure everything out? Why did Satan approach Eve rather than Adam in the beginning? There are many unanswered questions regarding the Fall, but through it, we can learn a great deal about the prince of darkness and his typical dealings with mankind. He goes straight for the jugular of the weakest link to create seeds of doubt. To verify, just take a trip back to the garden of Eden narrative or re-read Jesus' own dialogue with Satan in the wilderness.

When you're entrenched in a fiery spiritual battle, one thing is essential to remember. The unseen, all-important combat, contrary to many distracting modern philosophies, is still the age-old clash of ultimate Good versus "heavenly" evil. Just remember, it's God versus Satan, and no matter how it sometimes looks, evil is not, and never, ever will be, on par with the ultimate goodness of God. Satan knows this too, and in his hatred for all humans, both male and female, he is determined to make as many of us as possible believe in evil's supreme power for our ultimate demise. After all, he is a master manipulator—if it were not so, I doubt a third of heaven's angels would have been convinced to follow him on the initial (and ultimate) journey to hell.[36]

One of the best books on the inner mental workings of demonic spiritual warfare is *The Screwtape Letters* by C.S. Lewis. It is worthy of many a re-read, especially when you are in the midst of the incessant battle. If you are not familiar with the book, it takes a bit of getting used to, as it is a series of letters written from the perspective of a senior demon named Screwtape to a young recruit named Wormwood. The newbie has been assigned to a recently saved human in order to get him to doubt and eventually renounce his newfound faith. Screwtape, the author of the letters and the wiser fiend, always refers to God as the Enemy, and in the sample below, the label "vermin" is given to all mankind:

> Of course, I know that the Enemy also wants to detach men from themselves, but in a different way. Remember always that he really likes the little vermin and sets an absurd value on the distinctness of every one of them. When he talks of their losing themselves, he only means abandoning the clamor of self-will; once they have done that, He really gives them back all their personality and boasts (I am afraid, sincerely) that when they are wholly His, they will be more themselves than ever.[37]

My favorite reminder is found in "He really likes the little vermin and sets an absurd value on the distinctness of every one of them."

> *For God so loved the world that he gave his*
> *one and only Son, that whoever believes in*
> *him shall not perish but have eternal life.*
> John 3:16 (NKJV)

That, in a nutshell, is the rationale behind the cross. In that sense, gender is completely irrelevant. Just because such overarching love and devotion for a single individual are truly incomprehensible to the wee, finite human mind does not make it any less True. He has proven this concept over and over to me, and His individual love for each one of us is beyond description. Often, during those special moments when I am aware that I am prayerfully talking with someone simply as an empty vessel that He loves people through, it literally takes my breath away. If you really want to know how much He cares, just ask Him—and wait for His answer.

> *"Behold, I stand at the door and knock. If*
> *anyone hears my voice and opens the door,*
> *then I will come into him and will dine with*
> *him, and he with me."* Revelation 3:20
> (NKJV)

"If a man loves me, he will keep my words: and my Father will love him, and we will come unto him, and make our abode with him." John 14:23 (KJV)

Both verses are often used in reference to salvation, but when one examines the context closely, it is obvious that these passages are about believers deepening their enduring relationship with the triune God. Sadly, one is much slower to even hear the knock, let alone open the door, when life is comfortably good, and something interesting is on TV. Again, getting out of one's own predictable zone and trusting God with each step of life's journey changes everything.

Thus, I will always be most grateful for those early years in Kurdistan where, for a while, it was just He and I on an incredible adventure *together*...Spiritual awareness is the biggest blessing of cross-cultural service because one's urgent need for His ceaseless moment-by-moment presence is undeniable, and His faithful provision beyond compare, regardless of whether you are male or female.

***

To be sure, life for a single expatriate woman in the Middle East is often difficult and lonely, but life for a single Kurdish woman is excruciatingly tough. There is simply no place for them in society. Generally, In Kurdish culture, daughters are raised to be good wives, which is often synonymous with slaves, depending on the family. Sons, on the other hand, are frequently spoiled "princes," as they are always held in the highest regard as the family's future hope. Neither can leave their parents' house easily until they are married. One stays to serve, the other to be served. Generally, an unmarried woman eventually becomes like a spinster aunt and has to rely on the ongoing goodwill of male relatives. Any marriage, even a bad one, is often preferable.

Islam denotes a lesser status for women and teaches that they are in some ways a kind of evil, as they can distract a man from more important spiritual pursuits. Further, any woman's physical beauty is only meant to be enjoyed by her husband and thus the necessity for the various coverings. It has been my experience that Kurdish Muslim women, for the most part, have fully bought into this idea of inherent badness within, and they go to great lengths to protect their daughters from themselves.

Perpetuating this state of affairs is where the widespread acceptance came from of the horrific practice of genital mutilation, which still continues secretly in some parts of Kurdistan. It is not the fathers but the mothers and the aunts who hold down their precious six-year-old girls so that the clitoris can be completely removed—effectively and permanently eliminating any physical, sexual pleasure for the female. Thus, they are *protected*, as they would not ever be tempted to act on fleshly desires of their own and bring shame to the family.[38]

Moreover, the true status of women in Iraqi Kurdistan is often confounded by political maneuvers that outwardly look good but do nothing to change or even confront the wrong thinking. Female faith workers find this out the hard way. One woman, who lived with a young missionary couple and their three daughters from her sending organization, had planned a special evangelistic movie showing for a small group of university students that she had been working with for several months. She literally spent hours on the invitations, special treats, and other details in hopes of making it an incredibly special time for all. As the arrival hour came and went without the appearance of a single guest, the woman was puzzled and eventually quite despondent.

Here's where the ever-present spiritual warfare rushes in with a scratchy, whiny voice reverberating in one's head, berating you for absolutely everything. *"Obviously, you are not effective; what are you doing here? You are just a girl! You're not making a difference. Nobody wants you here; they would have come if they actually liked you…"* and so on and so forth—over and over and over. Again, this voice of lies from the eternal inferno never gives up its relentless attack on the front lines…except when you are in conversation with the Lord. The solution is simple enough: repeatedly talk it out with God, wherever you are. It takes a while, but eventually, with enough discussion and loving reminders of Truth, you come to see the humor in the most bizarre and initially hurtful situations.

Several days later, the woman stumbled upon the actual reality of the matter when one of the students casually asked her what had happened to the movie plan. It turned out that the students had indeed come by around the appointed time but were subsequently turned away by the house guard with the surprising news that no one was at home. The event happened to fall while the husband was away traveling, so in the minds of the local guards, since *only* women remained behind, there really was no one at home. The students accepted this, never thinking about calling to double check because that might shame their beloved teacher. When the woman eventually confronted the guard on the issue, he was completely appalled and saddened that she did not want the protection he had been trained to provide in the absence of the man of the house.

It is those kinds of mental misdemeanors that you have to especially watch out for in successful cross-cultural living. As a single gal serving in the Middle East, it is so easy to take exaggerated offense at the constant underlying non-person status assigned to all females, especially those unfortunate enough not to have "snagged" a husband along the way. As a middle-aged female to boot, I was even advised by my first cultural guide to just wear a ring and stretch the truth a bit. I never did, but I understood why it was a reasonable request. It simply boggles the mind of any national here, male or female, that a sane woman would actually choose a single lifestyle, thereby effectively forfeiting any real sense of identity. On the other hand, for fiercely independent 20th-century women of the west (like myself, for instance), who literally grew up on Helen Reddy's "I am a Woman, Hear me Roar" type mentality—such archaic, rigid thinking is completely unacceptable.

At least on a sub-conscious level, I am afraid that we automatically decide that this must be constantly addressed, often serving as an effective distraction to the actual work for which we have been commissioned. As female sinners in a fallen world, we naturally long for a sense of power and worth. Unfortunately, it is quite easy to mistake that inner yearning of the flesh for something much more spiritual in nature. At the end of the proverbial day, you cannot take yourself too seriously, and you need to purposefully practice rejoicing in small victories as they happen.

Winter in Kurdistan always means rain, and in villages or areas of new construction, like my apartment was, rain means mud—and plenty of it! Unfortunately, it is a gooey clay-like substance that not only sucks you in like quicksand but also tends to make the culturally all-important, spotlessly clean and shiny shoes an impossibility. When I faced that scenario daily for a season, I started putting plastic shopping bags over my shoes so that I could just throw the bags away when I made it to the paved street. At first, everybody stared in horror, but they generally do anyway, so I figured what the heck; at least my friends would not be saddened by the state of my muddy shoes. It was a small win, to be sure, but I have to admit I was pretty excited the day I noticed my neighbors doing the same thing. With a cheery smile and a wave, we all pointed at our feet with a giggle—talk about impacting worldview!

***

I did not realize just how deeply some Kurdish men's minds were entrenched in this same false reasoning of protecting women from themselves until I moved out to the rural area of Raparin and began to teach English and Critical Thinking at the university. Most of my students were highly educated men, and many of them were also married. One day we were discussing technological developments, and the idea of robots for the home was introduced. A few men immediately reacted negatively to such a prospect. They explained that such inventions would not be good for Kurdistan as those were the kinds of jobs that kept their wives busy, and it would be horrible if they did not have enough to do, as they would then become lazy and get themselves in trouble. My few female students rolled their eyes a bit but did not comment publicly. They did, however

119

seek me out privately, and I will always be thankful for the ongoing chances to comfort and nurture starving, oppressed young female hearts as only another woman can.

Furthermore, the circumstances were such in Iraqi Kurdistan that I was thrust into an unexpected ministry leadership role on the field as a divorced woman. In the beginning, I was simply "scouting" out the land as part of the boss's inner team. To be sure, he faced official heat for sending a woman alone to do even that in a place like Iraq. His own philosophy, though, was that a woman placed temporarily with a faith-based group could find out more about the actual situation in a culture where women were automatically viewed as lesser beings and thus would not be considered a substantial threat. I actually found that to be true, at least to a point. Also, an encouraging visit from a colleague soon followed. JT was a successful pastor turned message bearer who began the ominous task of remotely designing the best possible curriculum for our unique and multi-faceted students.

Once the Entrust program got started, we were operating a kind of portable Bible school in four different locations with classes taught as week-long intensives four times a year. For quite a while, I was the only one representing the organization on the ground during the interim times. Hence, for years, I found myself the sole female, by default, in meeting after meeting with government officials and various church leaders. I found it all quite exhausting. Men are weird…ask any woman! I am sure the opposite is true for them as well. Physical differences are obvious, but it goes beyond that to what is unseen. According to recent Stanford Medical research, new technologies have generated a growing pile of evidence that there are inherent differences in how men's and women's brains are wired and how they work.[39]

Additionally, we were blessed to have a faithful set of seasoned, dynamic male teachers and pastors who made the long and dangerous trip multiple times each year for the five-year program. Thus, I never tried to formally teach the Bible; it was clearly not necessary. The Christian-background female students were adamant that they wanted to be taught by the men, as it made it more official and real, especially at that time. So, in spite of the angst of a few western female colleagues, it was one battle I simply was not willing to take part in. The proper role of either women or divorced people in Christian ministry has been debated through the ages with excellent arguments, once again, on both sides... and lots of agreeing to disagree in the end. In my mind, it simply depends on prayer and the situation at hand.

At one point, we did offer a series of ladies' Bible classes primarily for the wives of our Kurdish students. The fellowship was a delight for all of us, but the women themselves gave up after a few months because they felt they were humiliating their husbands too much. Another rule of hospitality in Kurdistan is that you are always welcome to visit, even without warning. Of course, if you visit a man and his wife is not at home, it shames the man because he obviously is not taking charge of his woman properly. In this society, to bring shame on your immediate family is almost worse than murder. Hence, the most productive way to build strong ongoing relationships with married women is still through home visits, which take an enormous amount of energy and a great deal of time.

Likewise, there is a strange and sad phenomenon that continues to plague the worldwide mission field in terms of gender demographics. Seasoned message bearer, Nik Ripken, addresses this very issue in his recent book entitled *The Insanity of Obedience: Walking with Jesus in Tough Places:*

> Careful examination of the mission community reveals an intriguing reality—for every single man in overseas service, there are approximately seven single women. Why is this so?
>
> Does the heavenly Father have a communication problem with single men? Are single women simply easier to convince? Are single men reading past the biblical commands to go to the nations? Is it that God,

for some reason, needs more women than men?

One mission leader, grappling with this trend in his own areas of service, often addresses gatherings of college and seminary students. Many of these college students are single. He suggested to the single men that they need to cease praying the prayer that exclaims, "Here I am, Lord, send my sister!" That comment would be funny if it did not ring so true.

Even in the toughest places, even in places wracked by war and famine, single women within the mission community outnumber single men 7 to 1—that statistic seems consistent across denominational lines and within different areas of the world.[40]

Kurdistan has been no exception in this odd and discouraging trend, and single women struggle to be considered valuable even on their own teams—yet still, they come and faithfully plant seeds. To be sure, family is God's own picture of building a vibrant community, and that has not changed. I long and pray for the day when the treasured young Kurdish men God has entrusted to me for a short time are given a chance to walk beside godly men in fellowship and examine together their roles as husbands and fathers. I got a taste of such when two veteran American couples, the As and the Gs, joined our NGO staff in Raparin for a season. The lasting, miraculous difference a small community of believers on the ground makes, who are outward in their faith, is awe-inspiring. I believe it is a harvest waiting to happen. So, we continue to pray.

The arena of women ministering to other women in the larger faith community is a foreign concept for the most part. Married women in Kurdistan, regardless of religion, are remarkably busy. By far, the primary responsibility for all aspects of hospitality, house administration, child-rearing, and spiritual advancement of the family falls on the woman's shoulders. As many men will tell you, their wives are their "ministers of the interior" and often have tremendous control within the house. However, they are not encouraged at all to be part of society at large. Hence, the chances of young married women befriending others outside of their own relations are quite limited.

I was excited, therefore, to see the positive responses when we began to make various mixed-gender field trips with our non-profit service organization. For many of these young college graduates, it was the first time they had ever seen other parts of Kurdistan, and they found they actually liked such adventures and *each other* far beyond their own expectations.

I realized this opened the door for further opportunities to create gender-specific activities as well. The males already had options of a sort: sport, travel, and tea/hookah shops. For the girls, I knew we needed to get creative. So, when one of our female staff got engaged, I approached her about the idea of a bridal shower.

"What?" she said, her eyes growing large and frightened. "Do you really want to do that to me?" Her chin quivered a bit, and I saw what appeared to be tears gathering.

"Wait a minute, my dear, what exactly do you think a bridal shower is? Have you heard of them before?" I queried in bewilderment.

She nodded slowly and softly replied, "We don't do them here normally, but I have heard about what they do from friends in Turkey. It sounds scary and painful, but if you think I need one, then I trust you, as you are like a mother to me."

I gave her a quick hug and asked for more of a description of the Turkish practice she had heard about since I had never equated the idea of a bridal shower with either terror or pain. She went on to explain that the procedure involves several older ladies taking the young bride-to-be into the bathroom shower room where she is made to undress, and they then begin beating her with sticks and other objects.

"No," I said softy. "That is not at all what I had in mind. How about if we have a party instead, where we play silly games and give you gifts?"

"Oh," she exclaimed with a grin, "now that sounds fun!"...and it was.

***

Women need each other in a special way, especially in a place like Iraqi Kurdistan, where, as a woman, you never know who to trust. No matter what, when something immoral has happened, it is always the girl's fault in the eyes of rural Kurdish society. Often the nuclear family bows to the incessant pressure and turns on the girl as well. Further, if it is a case of incest or abuse, no one will turn to the authorities because, historically, they will just defer to the man of the house, who is often the abuser himself. Hence the rate of suicide among young women is truly abhorrent and seldom talked about. There are so many challenges and difficulties of life for a female that only another woman, or God Himself, can relate to and empathize with. Gender-wise, we are indeed uniquely different but equally and overwhelmingly loved by a Creator who understands each heart and has no limits.

In an encouraging sign, I have also seen, just in the last few years, a new yearning for a vibrant women's ministry among the various groups of followers scattered throughout the wider region that I have become acquainted with over the last few decades. I continue to pray for the vision to be captured and acted upon by younger, married female leaders in the area and beyond. I think, in time, women of the Middle East and elsewhere, with their unique God-given giftings, could become important bridges to all aspects of societal understanding and spiritual growth.

Chapter Seven: It's "Complexicated"

Solving a jigsaw puzzle when the pieces keep changing shapes.

To this day, Kurdistan remains an incredibly special slice in a bizarre puzzle, where each spiritual, political, and individual piece seems to have the unique ability to alter its shape at will. If you like jigsaw puzzles, you can understand just how infuriating that event would be. Equipping leaders for Kingdom service in such an atmosphere remained a constant exercise in frustration that continually led us back to the Prince of Peace and our utter dependence on Him. That is actually a good thing—it just doesn't always feel that way.

The situation was made much more convoluted by all the characteristics of life and relationships in a fallen world during constant change, war, and unremitting uncertainty. Moreover, the larger region is a geographical area well known for its vast oil wealth as well as the territory that could be considered "the holy grail" of three major world religions. Every time I turned around, it seemed that I was completely confused and often despondent—just where God wanted me.

Likewise, for the first four years of the project, I was still heavily involved in the home office administration as well as dealing on a regular basis with my parents' failing health, so I often felt like I met myself coming and going. This phenomenon was seldom pretty. Only people who have experienced in-and-out cross-cultural living understand the incredible frustration of always feeling misunderstood and a bit ostracized in both locales. It was probably similar to how the Son of Man (Jesus' favorite title for himself) felt as he traveled continuously during his three years of ministry. Geographically, he only went as far as He could travel by foot, and yet he faced a wide assortment of differing cultural norms at every turn.[41]

As a team, we eventually realized that there are no pat answers or one-size-fits-all approaches or methods. I believe that such has never been God's intention, no matter how marvelous it sounds in an annual board meeting. We began purposefully looking for ways to give the national leaders an equal voice and a sense of camaraderie. We determined to listen better. Progress was excruciatingly slow; we realized that the job was far from over, and the chance of healthy multiplication within a generation dimmed.

It continues to take a great deal more time and prayer than the strategic planner types anticipate. There remains an immense spirit of fear, divisiveness, age-old grudge-bearing, and general hopelessness that hangs over the land in an almost palpable manner, contaminating every corner of life and relationship. Undeniably, just as "Ahmed" pointed out, it's also essential for western workers to realize that the foundational guilt-and-innocence grid through which we view the world culturally is much different than that of many eastern cultures, who look at life from the standpoints of shame and honor, or fear and power, or some combination of both.

Jayson Georges produced a concise book on the issue entitled *The 3D Gospel: Ministry in Guilt, Shame and Fear Cultures.* He plainly illustrates examples of each culture type with compelling stories and instances from the Word that demonstrate how God brings truth to bear in captivating ways for each and every different worldview and how we, as disciples, need to do the same. As Georges points out using the book of Ephesians, God's Word consistently speaks to all three worldviews, but everybody tends to emphasize that which speaks most openly to their own core beliefs.[42]

As His message bearers, we need to consciously realize this and practice rightly dividing the Word in such a way that our disciples and disciples-to-be see God's sovereignty and eternal solution for themselves—wherever they are and however they think.

Seeing the Complete Diamond

As Georges observes:

The gospel is a many-sided diamond, and God wants people in all cultures to experience his complete salvation. But despite the multifaceted nature of Christian salvation, Western Christianity emphasizes one aspect of salvation (i.e., the forgiveness of sins), thus neglecting other facets of the gospel of Jesus Christ. Imagine a diamond with only one side! For cross-cultural workers, a truncated gospel hinders spirituality, theology, relationships, and ministry. We unintentionally put God in a box, only allowing him to save in one arena.[43]

Our ever-changing "advancing" global society is now creating cultures within cultures within cultures, and I submit that nobody has it totally right when it comes to an understanding of emerging worldviews. The millennials in America seem to understand the millennials in Kurdistan better than either understand my own generation or vice versa. Being human, every faith worker would naturally like to claim that "aha" place in the sun of accurately defining a target culture's best chance of fully comprehending and receiving the Good News of Jesus Christ.

The problem is, the true "AH, HA" can come from nowhere but God Himself, and it's been my ongoing experience that He never relinquishes that position. Our aim should be to fully utilize the wonderful guidelines provided these days, but to do so prayerfully, always listening expectantly for God's own directive. Occasionally, He may alter your path in a bizarre way that makes no sense to any human strategy—trust His heart and remember, as Hebrews 13:8 points out so plainly, He is not the one that changed.

***

Fairly early on, it became all too obvious that being involved in our Entrust Kurdistan project could indeed be likened to raising children—VERY different children at that. Our Arabic-speaking Christian-background study groups were like hungry bookworm types who devoured anything we gave them in the intensive courses. They gladly met weekly (or even more frequently) between sessions just to engage in lively and rich discussion on spiritual matters for at least a couple of hours. It's critical here to remember that Christian-background folks already venerated the Bible, trusted its contents, and had legal permission AND social encouragement to practice Christianity. Moreover, our students were all first-generation departures from Catholicism and Orthodoxy and were determined to probe scripture carefully to prove, among other things, the rightness of their move into Protestantism.

The other groups were made up solely of Kurdish speakers of Muslim or folk religion backgrounds. While they were only five hours away by car (the Christian background group met in Duhok and the Kurdish group in Sulaymaniah, opposites sides of the Kurdistan region), the people themselves tended to travel in a different hemisphere altogether. Our Kurdish brothers' usually animated eyes were quick to glaze over at the very mention of the word "study," and they would much rather spend the time teaching you how to dance or planning the next picnic on the mountain. God graciously gave everyone involved here a fierce love and deep respect for all of the members of each group—it's just the "process" that got a tad confusing at times.

Highly educated theologians have willingly sacrificed various amounts of their lives in the fields of places like Kurdistan, and they are often bursting with gems of intellect and differing doctrinal issues to share. Sovereignty versus free will and the gifts of the Holy Spirit often rise to the top of the list, just like they do in our own country. Entrust teachers regularly attempted to share the other schools of thought on "secondary" matters, but if we are honest with ourselves, that is always subjective, and one's own bias, as well as that of the translator being used, usually shines through and often serves as a hindrance. As one seasoned *residential* Bible teacher put it:

"The fact is that when you are teaching through a translator unless you know well the language being translated into, you have no way to be sure exactly what is being said! A few times, I was told, 'When you said this, he actually said this!' And I would think, 'Oh, no! God help us!'"[44]

The reason *residential* is in italics above is because I have found that it's essential to even knowing when the truth is being misaligned through translation. Often it wasn't that the student didn't have enough English to understand there was a difference, but they would just never share it publicly until they trusted you enough to speak with you privately. That is the kind of life-on-life impact that only happens with time and continued presence.

Thus, we must pick our theological battles very carefully, just as Jesus modeled and the Apostles eventually followed. For evangelical intellectuals, it is sometimes painfully hard to let go of certain theological rabbit trails that they have spent significant time exploring and want all to be as excited as they are about the uniqueness of their pet nuggets. Inadvertently, this can cloud the compelling simplicity of the gospel story—especially when you are dealing primarily with ethnic groups that have been repressed for generations. Such was, and still is to a large extent, the case of overt believers in Kurdistan—just as it was in Galilee so long ago. They tend to misread even the simplest analogies, at least in the beginning. It is encouraging to remember that Jesus Himself used simple everyday objects to teach eternal lessons to his disciples, and still they often got it totally wrong at first.

Consider, for instance, chapter 16:6 of Matthew's Gospel, when Jesus warns his followers to beware of the yeast of the Pharisees and Sadducees. Right away, when the men talk among themselves, they decide He is displeased with them because they had forgotten to bring bread on this trip. These are the same guys who, not once but twice, had just witnessed the miracle of Jesus actually feeding thousands with a few fish and loaves!

> *But Jesus, being aware of it, said to them, "O you of little faith, why do you reason among yourselves because you have brought no bread? Do you not yet understand or remember the five loaves of the five thousand and how many baskets you took up? Nor the seven loaves of the four thousand and how many large baskets you took up? How is it you do not understand that I did not speak to you concerning bread?—but to beware of the leaven of the Pharisees and Sadducees." Then they understood that He did not tell them to beware of the leaven of bread but of the doctrine of the Pharisees and Sadducees.*
>
> Matthew 16:8-12 (NKJV)

Max Lucado also offers a humorous but compelling story regarding this same convoluted situation. It is a popular story among believers in Iraq, as it examines the inherent danger when we do not keep matters straightforward and fail to let the one and only Bread of Life speak for Himself through prayer, ongoing relationship, and careful Bible study.

The Beggar and the Bread

A beggar came and sat before me. "I want bread," he said.

"How wise you are!" I assured him. "Bread is what you need. And you have come to the right bakery." So, I pulled my cookbook down from my shelf and began to tell him all I knew about bread.

I spoke of flour and wheat, grain and barley. My knowledge impressed even me as I cited the measurements and recipe. When I looked up, I was surprised to see he wasn't smiling. "I just want bread," he said.

"How wise you are!" I applauded his choice. "Follow me, and I'll show you our bakery." Down the hallowed halls, I guided him, pausing to point out the rooms where the dough is prepared and the ovens where the bread is baked.

"No one has such facilities. We have bread for every need. But here is the best part," I proclaimed as I pushed open two swinging doors. "This is our room of inspiration." I knew he was moved as we stepped into the auditorium full of stained-glass windows.

The beggar didn't speak. I understood his silence. With my arm around his shoulder, I whispered, "It overwhelms me as well." I then leaped to the podium and struck my favorite pose behind the lectern. "People come from miles to hear me speak. Once a week, my workers gather, and I read to them the recipe from the cookbook of life."

By now, the beggar had taken a seat in the front row. I knew what he wanted. "Would you like to hear me?"

"No," he said, "but I would like some bread."

"How wise you are!" I replied. And I led him to the front door of the bakery. "What I have to say next is very important," I told him as we stood outside. "Up and down this street, you will find many bakeries. But take heed, they don't serve the true bread. I know of one who adds two spoons of salt rather than one. I know of another whose oven is three degrees too hot. They may call it bread," I warned. "But it's not according to the book."

The beggar turned and began walking away. "Don't you want bread?" I asked him.

He stopped, looked back at me, and shrugged, "I guess I lost my appetite."

I shook my head and returned to my office. "What a shame!" I said to myself. "The world just isn't hungry for true bread anymore."

I don't know what is more incredible: that God packages the bread of life in the wrapper of a country carpenter or that he gives us the keys to the delivery truck. Both moves seem pretty risky. The carpenter did his part, however. And who knows—we may just learn to do ours.[45]

There is only one perfect "bakery," and by God's grace, one day, we will experience it fully together, just as Jesus promised. Meanwhile, our primary task remains the same that He employed: go where He leads and do good, making disciples by pointing people toward a meaningful relationship with God, day after day after day.

At this point in world history, it is vital to wrestle with exactly what our job is as God's kids. What a different place Earth might be if His followers focused solely on living life in the same manner that Jesus did. Beware, governments won't like it, politicians won't like it, and sadly many prominent church boards and ministry leaders will despise it as well. After all, look at what those in religious authority did when Jesus walked the earth. There was definitely a comparable "religious right"—they just happened to be Jewish at the time and were the only group of all the different types of people that Jesus routinely interacted with that He clearly had no patience with.[46]

Moreover, it is obvious throughout the different gospel accounts that many of the disciples hoped that Jesus would eventually rule politically.[47] Well-known historical fiction writer Taylor Caldwell, in the book *I, Judas,* even tackled the possibility that such wrong thinking was the basis behind Judas's betrayal—a Satan-fueled, misguided push to forcefully launch Jesus into a place of power politically. It is a tough pill to swallow for most as the story actually makes a compelling case. In that sense, it easily could have been any one of us. His own responses, though, always came back to a focus on the present invisible rule of God within our individual lives. If we are honest enough with ourselves in the spiritual realm, we need to look in the "mirror" and prayerfully ask for a clear reflection of our own motivations and priorities in all work that we do in His name.

****

As the years went by in Kurdistan, I began to more fully empathize with the grumbling that Moses endured so long ago as he was bringing the children of Israel out of Egypt. Uncertainty is so brutally exhausting, and sometimes a past where you had no choices looks downright inviting, even if it was actually slavery and oppressive tyranny. Further, as new outrages rose up from various unexpected corners within, the Kurdish people's collective memories of Saddam softened quite a bit, and you began to hear statements like: "Saddam was a vicious monster with those who crossed him, but he was also a brilliant leader for those who obeyed. He took better care of us than our own Kurdish government does now. He never missed salaries, and there was no crime."

Criminality was actually fairly non-existent because, under the Saddam regime, even stealing an apple would routinely result in the removal of one's hand. Certainly, you do not have to go far these days to find many superbly written accounts of the horrifying, genocidal atrocities leveled against the Kurdish race by Saddam Hussein time and again. The trouble is that, for the most part, the younger generation of Kurds, often encouraged by their parents not to, do not study their own history. This is another blunder of colossal proportion, but sadly, not exactly an unexpected mistake when it comes to the general Kurdish passivity and heartfelt desire for all to be lasting sweetness and light, especially for their children.

I will always remember the extended discussions as an elementary school teacher trainer on the implementation of fire drills as a safety precaution. The majority of the staff were opposed to such an idea. They did not feel it was necessary to scare the children in that way as they believed buildings of brick and mortar do not burn, at least not in Kurdistan. Why put ideas of trouble in their innocent heads was the constant question. I even brought up a bomb scare scenario, which definitely gave the teachers pause, but it was not enough to convince them to prepare their young students for proper rescue and evacuation; it might frighten them.

Kurdish adults in their forties and beyond have lived with that incessant, hope-killing anxiety their entire lives, and they desperately want something different for their children. But sadly, history does have a habit of repeating itself, and stuffing one's personal trauma deep below the surface only prolongs the inevitable, often in dangerous ways.

***

"What is a typical day like for you?" is still the most common question I get during stateside reporting. In truth, life in Kurdistan is almost always atypical, despite the best-laid plans. Interruptions, crises of all kinds, and last-minute alterations are the continual norm. At one point, I created a pictorial analogy of daily existence here that remains apt even now. It's much like a complex roller coaster ride that never actually ends. Actually, I happen to like roller coaster rides – after all, they do not generally make me nauseous, and they're full of chug, chug, chug, climbing anticipation, followed by a thrilling whoosh—a twisting drop that leaves you breathless and just thankful to be alive.

Admittedly the thrill itself can be good or bad, but regardless, it is still a thrill. Join me for a spell on the type of disjointed ride that still continues to take place inside my head as I go about the daily tasks that seem so simple in a world where everything tends to work:

CHUG, CHUG, CHUG... Lord, I am so glad that I have just moved into a small apartment with F's precious family now living below, to help me figure out how to "catch" the city water between 5 and 9 AM every other day (important so we can fill up our rooftop water tank) and why only our breaker (the one on the end) pops off every ten minutes or so, regardless of what we do or don't turn on when the community generator is being used. This basically means a trip down the street each time with a broom handle to manually flip it back up—so we all take turns while the neighbors watch, adding special meaning to the new-kids-on-the-block mentality.

We could buy more amps, but at this point, we are not really sure it would make a difference. Stretching money is an issue in everything these days here—just since my initial arrival in March of 2004, medium-quality petrol has gone from around 6 cents a gallon to over $4.00 a gallon. A kilo of non-rotten tomatoes has gone from under a dollar to over three. Rent has gone from an average of $2-300 for a modest 2-bedroom house to about $800 and up (way, way up for the new apartments with the fancy stuff)—the list goes on and on...

WHOOOOSH... "Yes, it's true," the doctor calmly told me. "There is a significant outbreak of cholera here. What people don't understand, though, is that there have been outbreaks of cholera in the fall in this area for decades as the safe water sources dry up—we just didn't tend to call it that until now, and we didn't use to be in a spotlight of world news." He shrugged his shoulders, "It's just the way it is. I am actually more concerned from a medical standpoint by the increasing cases of Malta Fever, otherwise known as Brucellosis, as we have yet to pinpoint its cause..."

CHUG, CHUG, CHUG... As I drive around town, I am encouraged. Drivers actually take turns occasionally; bypasses and traffic signals are operational, and major building projects are being completed. More women are seen behind the wheel on a regular basis, and city power (you know, the kind where you can wash clothes, blow dry hair, vacuum, etc.) is more plentiful and on a nearly reliable schedule—not just at 3 AM. Kurdistan is progressing, albeit slowly... Quality goods and services are becoming available, oil drilling is beginning to take place, and the towns are expanding...

WHOOSH... Did you hear the news? Yesterday an Iranian businessman officially invited to Suly by the Kurdish government was snatched by the US military in plainclothes in a suspected terrorist sting operation at the Palace Hotel.

"They didn't even ask us," high officials heatedly lamented. "What is democratic about that? Just who do they think they are?"

Remember, in a shame/honor society failing to protect your guests is the worst kind of failure. So much for my coffee shop office with the free internet and a blight on the favored past status of the red, white, and blue...

CHUG, CHUG, CHUG... My own prayer life is always enhanced by random taxi rides between cities to the various provinces where we work—nothing like a little bumper-to-bumper tailgating at 120 km/hour to pointedly remind me of Who must be in control. (Nah, that does not qualify as a "whoosh"—just a little burp in the chug...)

All in all, the Entrust study groups are going exceptionally well, and despite ongoing challenges, we are hearing incredible, heartwarming reports of growing maturity, widespread conversions, and continued hunger for spiritual truth. Accurate oral and written translation for further study remains our biggest obstacle in this land where the whole Tower of Babel-speaking in tongues principle is magnified beyond belief.

At the dinner table, for instance, I now hear lots of words I do not recognize. In explanation, F tells me his Sorani is a bit weak since they often speak Hawrami (the Kakai dialect of Kurdish) in the home, and his schooling was in Arabic, whereas his wife's was in Farsi... confused yet? Welcome to my world...

WHOOSH... One chain of banks (a new novelty in itself) in the region has frozen all accounts – word on the street is they loaned out too much money by mistake... A pastor was recently unexpectedly jailed for a week for not properly registering his church outreach work. A fairly easy mistake to make since registration regulations at the moment change on a daily, if not hourly, basis. It turns out that he was actually turned in by another believer who was jealous and wanted him to get in trouble but did not think they would actually jail him. However, he reports that he was treated very well in jail and ended up leading a couple of other prisoners to the Lord... sound familiar?

Then there is the report of a new form of copycat terrorism taking hold in some villages. One corrupt mayor of a small town on the road to Baghdad has decided to play both hero and villain. He has people kidnapped, and then after whatever of value is coerced out of their terrified families, he "rescues" the abducted, and they are returned unharmed, minus their life savings.

CHUG, CHUG, CHUG... the more I study the history of this area, the more I realize just how complexicated it all is (since I am currently dealing in so many languages, I thought I should go ahead and make up some new English words while I am at it). There is obviously a lot going on behind the scenes, and we occasionally hear of actions on the part of the secret police and sometimes even that of the secret, secret police (yes, there actually are two branches). Checkpoints take a lot longer now, and any foreign IDs are heavily scrutinized. Moreover, there is more Kurdish military presence in Suly than I have seen in a long time, and there is a multitude of warnings from locals not to be out after dark as that is when horrible things tend to happen.

WHOOSH... At the end of the day, it's still better to laugh than cry. In the midst of it all, everyone needs a chuckle now and then to reduce the ever-present stress, if only for a moment. Sadly, the one item that rarely translates successfully is humor. For instance, the other day, some of the brothers were practically rolling on the floor and wanted to share the joke with me. So, between hilarious guffaws, they explained about the time the herd of sheep crossed the road, and one got hit by a passing truck. The sheep was thought to be dead but turned out only to have a bad concussion. When it woke up, however, it stood shakily to its feet and, to the surprise of all, began to "meow" …years later, when I tell this same joke to my young Kurdish staff, it still produces ample laughter that I have yet to really understand.

That same night a total stranger walked up to me at a traffic stop and, after affirming that I was an American, adamantly insisted on giving me a bit of money in order to take flowers to his beloved Thomas Edison's grave the next time I was in the States…such is life in Kurdistan—chug, chug, chug!

***

Party politics on all sides is another distraction that constantly interferes with any lasting improvement. As the revered Bush administration departed, there was a growing sense among the Kurdish people that American plans had turned against them once again. Kurdistan in those days was its own peculiar little universe with extraordinarily little awareness of the outside world, for the most part. They did tend to stop on a regular basis and watch a bit of what our government was doing, however.

Thus, the U.S. presidential election of 2008 was of great interest. As usual, skewed media presentation works well on both sides of the ocean. I saw a certain clip shown repeatedly for months. It was from one of the political commercials where Barack Obama's face appears, and you cannot hear what he's saying until he says the line, "The Bush-McCain policies of the last eight years have completely failed." Unfortunately, this came out loud and abundantly clear to the ears of this ethnic group, as they felt strongly that their own newly born sense of liberation resulted from those same "failed" policies. Hence, once again, just because I was American, I was asked by Kurdish people on the street why the USA did not believe that they were worth fighting for anymore.

Then 2009 rolled around, the second election year in the autonomous region itself that I had the opportunity to witness. Sadly, it was vastly different from the thankful, jubilant, and unified air of the 2005 election. Instead, there was much talk of rampant corruption, broken promises, and the need for change. As is probably always true in politics, there was also a great deal of back-room negotiating going on, but I had to laugh quietly when I heard of one instance where four rather obscure parties joined together as one to gain strength. One of the parties was a radical Islamic group, one was Reformed moderates, one was Communist, and the other a Socialist party...hmm, it is little wonder that they never were quite able to agree on a unified ideological platform.

I was also saddened to talk to a few friends who had already decided not to vote as they argued that it would not make any difference. It seemed the fatal disease of apathy was already slowly creeping into this distinctive land.

On the other hand, Kurds in general love a party and the pre-election process always provides a welcomed excuse. In Sulaymaniyah, banners flew in every direction, and each night several of the main streets were filled with campaign speeches, dancing, and youthful revelers engaged in their own form of drag racing. Admittedly, emotions ran so high that it was unnerving, and it also was unsettling when I learned that there were actually 28 different political parties vying for the coveted rule and 521 candidates to fill a mere 111 seats.

In the end, the status quo majority under the leadership of Masoud Barzani retained overarching control once more. All in all, the continued post-election peace was perhaps the greatest victory for the region. Considering the history of immediate and brutal violence among opposing Kurdish parties in the past, their current ability to accept defeat peacefully at this stage and regroup for the next time was truly a benchmark at the time in the region's overall development. Furthermore, the vast improvement over previous summers in available power and water was another indication that a bit of real progress, rather than momentary political back rubbing, was actually being made...at least until ISIS showed up...

Politics and religion are intricately related in this area of the world, and the ongoing wicked complexity of it all overwhelmed me at times—How could any individual discover Jesus for themselves and the reality of heaven in the midst of all these layers of ongoing muck and mistrust? I sometimes forgot just how consumed one becomes here in the roller coaster ups and downs of daily life, and by and large, the rest of the physical world often seemed kind of fuzzy and remote. The spiritual world, on the other hand, with all of its vicious, underhanded battles, clearly orchestrated by the Prince of Darkness, was right there in your face at every turn.

Satan is not all-knowing. Only God himself is omniscient and can actually read our minds.[48] However, the devil and his demons want you to believe otherwise and are consummate record keepers repeatedly striving hard to hit your weak areas, whatever they are. They rather brilliantly can recall previous failures then peck away at them like a prize fighter flicking at a cut over his opponent's eye. Hence, the need for intentionally putting on the *full* armor of God is critical.[49] The continual reassurance that prayer warriors literally have your back was, and still is, much more than a comfort beyond description—it's absolutely essential for long-term survival on the front lines. I say it all the time. I just wish the majority of the American church, in particular, genuinely believed it.

During this same time, I was introduced to the prolific work of bestselling author Joel C. Rosenburg. Joel is best known for his fictional work, which over the last couple of decades has seemed almost prophetic in nature. Many of his various plots have come true and continue to do so. He has also authored two excellent non-fiction books about the situation in the Middle East.

Their titles give concise hints as to where he is headed, and the books do not disappoint. The first was published in 2006, entitled *Epicenter: Why the Current Rumblings in the Middle East Will Change Your Future*. This was followed a few years later by his most extensive work, *Inside The Revolution: How the Followers of Jihad, Jefferson, & Jesus are Battling to Dominate the Middle East and Transform the World*.

I wholeheartedly recommend them both to anyone who really wants to know the various philosophies behind what was happening in this area of the world during the first decade of the 21st century. Joel is the "big picture guy" reporting on a gigantic forest with exceptional writing and research skills as well as biblical insight based on his own faith. To be sure, he gives a vital voice to many fairly unheard-of "characters" that continue to faithfully remove rocks, plant seeds, nurture growth and occasionally experience a harvest among the various trees. I found myself nodding again and again as his research and experiences in

Iraq, in particular, resonated so closely with my own. It was such an encouragement to understand that we were not alone in our strange little cabbage patch of Iraqi Kurdistan.

One particular section is part of what he calls the "Big, Untold Story," where he focuses country by country on the unprecedented revival that has been happening throughout the Middle East and Central Asia. Below he captures the thoughts of a prominent ministry leader in the south of Iraq that echoes what so many of us were seeing firsthand and hearing much about concerning Iran as well. In the end, the true hero of the story is still God and God alone—a point that sadly so often seems missing in the bigger missiological world:

> "Why such spiritual hunger?" Every Iraqi Christian I have interviewed has given me the same two answers: war and persecution. Though the security in Iraq was deteriorating from 2003 to 2007, one of the top leaders of the revivalist movement there told me he had never seen so many Iraqis praying to receive Christ and wanting Bible teaching. I asked him how he accounted for such developments.
>
> "It's not that complicated really, Joel," he replied. "When human beings are under threat, they look for a strong power to help

them—a refuge. Iraqis look around, and when they see believers in Jesus enjoying internal peace during a time of such violence and fear, they want Jesus too."

"But," I asked, "How did he and his disciples share their faith and lead people to Christ with all the suicide bombings, car bombings, snipers, and other troubles of the past few years?"

"We did what we could," he said. "But God is not dependent upon us. This is something He is doing on His own. He is drawing Muslims to Christ. We are just His servants, helping where we can. The truth is, that God is healing Muslims of sickness and diseases. He is also giving Muslims visions of Jesus Christ. He is coming to them and speaking to them, and they are repenting and giving their lives to Him. I'm saying that Shiites are seeing visions of Christ and repenting. When we meet them, they already believe in Jesus. We don't have to share the Gospel with them. We want to, but it's not necessary. They're already convinced that Jesus is the Savior... But you see, Joel, it is

God who is at work. He is making this happen—not us."[50]

Such stories continually challenged and refined my thinking regarding what it takes to be an effective message bearer in the 21st century. By 2010, huge shifts were happening in the worldwide body. Astounding reports of massive movements in some of the most resistant places on earth were and are being verified. Ignited by purposeful petition and lovingly sustained by the Comforter, the amazing transformation of entire communities continues. Such has not happened in Kurdistan…yet.

We did see a milder version of such revival within our region. However, it has never been of the magnitude described above. Perhaps it is because we have remained a relatively safe sanctuary all throughout those years. From a human standpoint, it seems the opposite should be true, but it is not. The tougher the pressure, the greater the life change.

Make no mistake, following the advent of Operation Iraqi Freedom, national believers in Kurdistan regularly experienced persecution, but not the kind that makes sensational news. It was often in the form of incessant, sometimes violent bullying, withheld medical treatment, intimidation, family threats, job demotion or loss, as well as occasional "safe" imprisonment rather than torture or execution. Moreover, in terms of sustainable employment, it was not always their newfound faith at the root of the problem. Sometimes, sadly, it was their own irresponsibility or basic laziness.

Further, I have found that, as scary as it sounds, jail or prison in Kurdistan often operates as a quick-fix band-aid until the authorities figure out what is actually going on. Those in charge are also quick to say, regarding Christians, that they often incarcerate them for their own safety and protection against the radicalized elements. I have actually seen that to be true…to be honest, the ones who suffer the most are the beloved family and co-workers on the outside facing society's harsh censure.

One such situation concerned one of our student leaders. We received word early one Sunday morning that our dear friend Pastor K in Duhok was taken without warning from his home by a special branch of the security police force. Extraordinarily little was known at first, other than that he was being moved frequently from one government facility to another. It had been unofficially acknowledged that he was being held in reference to a classified security matter and that the detention had nothing to do with his church work.

I immediately traveled the five hours to be with his wife, K, an incredibly special sister who was holding up remarkably well in spite of the circumstances. She simply asked me to urge everyone to pray that the Lord would somehow receive glory for the situation and that all believers in Kurdistan would remember that we are not given a spirit of fear. I will always remember the incredible joy in K's voice when she told me about finally being allowed to see her husband after almost 72 hours of not even knowing where he was being held. She then admitted that the previous few days had been some of the hardest of her life.

The first words out of her husband's mouth were, "I am fine. Did you bring my Bible?" She had, along with a comfortable mattress and lots of goodies. She was finally convinced then that, indeed, he was receiving excellent care as well as unprecedented opportunities to share his faith with the guards and other authorities—much like the apostle Paul did in the book of Acts.

The official story finally came out concerning the security matter. Pastor K and 24 other people were named by the parents in a rather ludicrous child abduction case that had first opened over a year previously. It went something like this. There was an extremely poor and rather infamous family in one of the outlying villages that Pastor K visited on a regular basis. Two years previously, he remembered visiting the family with a basket of food and some money for heating supplies and such. He recalled being very saddened because the man obviously suffered from mental illness, and the woman was well known as a kind of a modern-day Gomer (unfaithful wife of Old Testament prophet Hosea).

There were several small children there as well, and the woman made a comment at that time that she wished there was someone to take her sons away as they ate too much food and were a lot of trouble.

Pastor K tried valiantly to convince her that children were a miraculous blessing from the Lord to be treasured, but he did not feel like she was really listening and so was not overly surprised when he was told a few months later that she had actually sold one of her sons. Thus, when he had first learned of the "case," he thought it was some kind of a joke, and when he heard nothing else, he forgot about it. Basically, the mother had reported to the police that one of her sons had somehow been "lost," and she gave all these names of people who might have taken him, probably hoping to get some sort of additional money. The list included Pastor K.

Now for the unofficial story. First, much to their own grief, K & K are childless. Not only does that make them somewhat shunned in society here, but it also unfairly means that either would be immediately suspect anytime there is a case involving a missing child. Additionally, the month before, many believers, including Pastor K, had been involved in a widespread Christian tract circulation. The visiting American group behind the circulation had translated it into both Sorani and Behdini Kurdish, a story that ties Newroz, the Kurdish New Year, which falls on the first day of spring, March 21st, and is by far the most popular holiday in Kurdistan, to new life in Jesus and the Easter message.

Done in the right way, it could have provided a lasting link for Kurdish seekers. Unfortunately, it was written in the harsh, hateful language of the "turn or burn" philosophy. These tracts, along with those delightful little well-known shoe boxes that were being distributed all over the Duhok area, caused ripplings of great concern for certain religious powers that be. Hmm, how do you spell harassment and fear tactics? K was eventually released unharmed, but it would not be the first time that I watched short-term foreign faith workers create huge difficulties and leave our dear national brothers and sisters "holding the bag" of retribution and facing the hard, lonely work of prayerfully processing such ordeals alone. It must be why Jesus does expect us actually to be there moment by moment to love, faithfully and well, those temporarily entrusted to us, just as He did.

***

Another piece in the ever-changing faith puzzle was a significant influx of Arabic-speaking Christians, who were accepted and readily welcomed. The KRG knew that part of its ongoing survival as an autonomous region had to do with its ability to continue to serve as a bastion of religious freedom and a haven for non-Muslim minorities. Catholic, Orthodox, and Protestant churches have slowly flourished in the bigger cities, and they are able to worship without any fear of official reprisal. The region has a long way to go to achieve any sense of true equality, but they continue to take baby steps in the right direction.

Overall conversion and church growth within Iraqi Kurdistan IS happening—just in faltering measures, plagued with division and distrust. What has been most remarkable, however, is the ever-growing number of unchurched Kurdish believers in both Iraq and Iran that are adamant and vocal in their love for Jesus Christ and the gift of salvation. They just do not want ANYTHING to do with the organized church within Kurdistan, as they are convinced it is corrupt beyond repair, just like everything else in their world. Further, they believe that they are already following the biblical mandate to assemble, as many of them have led their entire family to faith in Jesus, and they regularly pray and read the Bible together. "When we have a question, we pray and ask God." I meet them in city bazaars or in remote villages, or on country roads, sometimes even literally from behind bushes on a hiking trail. It is weird, messy, and impossible to quantify, but isn't that just like God?

Meanwhile, life is changing at breakneck speed across the planet, and almost everyone, everywhere, seems to be numbly succumbing to the constant onslaught of high-stress busyness that envelopes us all. Everyone, that is, but Jesus. He is a multitude of complexity, and yet, He is still Jesus, the same yesterday, today, and forever. Faith, in a nutshell, simply means actively believing that He is the Way, the Truth, and the Life and that He has taught us how to live for the future if only we will. What else actually matters? It seems that the more convoluted a situation is, the more God's hand is clearly evident. Perhaps that is the point.

Chapter Eight: All That Glitters

Searching for the best when the good is so distracting

As the years rolled by, life in Kurdistan continued to be full of surprises and constant change. The second decade of the new millennium dawned, and the whole region was clearly rattling along at an even greater frenzied pace, tripping over chaos, corruption, and even the occasional success story. It was quite clear that no one really knew where we were all going at that point, but regardless, we were sure in a hurry to get there. Huge construction projects abounded in all the major cities, and store shelves expanded and brimmed with every conceivable gadget and gizmo promising to improve one's life for the better—batteries not included, of course.

Unfortunately, while the region surged forward economically, socially, and politically, it slowly became somewhat stagnant spiritually. Underlying fear, nationalistic pride, division, and discouragement continued a tyrannical rule in the hearts of the people. Meanwhile, a sense of deserved privilege and greed began to snuff out the attitude of gratitude that had so defined the area at the ushering in of the 21st century. As we get deeper into our technological age, there is no hiding how the ultra-rich life comes right into one's living room these days, and greener grass elsewhere is a constant mantra carefully crafted by the evil one as the only answer.

The cheerful little girl with bouncy golden curls was almost five. Waiting with her mother at the checkout stand, she saw them, a circle of glistening white pearls in a pink foil box.

"Oh, Mommy, please, Mommy. Can I have them? Please, Mommy, please?"

Quickly the mother checked the back of the little foil box and then looked back into the pleading blue eyes of her little girl's upturned face.

"A dollar ninety-five. That's almost $2.00. If you really want them, I'll think of some extra chores for you, and in no time, you can save enough money to buy them for yourself. Your birthday's only a week away, and you might get another crisp dollar bill from Grandma."

As soon as Jenny got home, she emptied her penny bank and counted out 17 pennies. After dinner, she did more than her share of chores, and she went to the neighbor and asked Mrs. McJames if she could pick dandelions for ten cents. On her birthday, Grandma did give her another new dollar bill, and at last, she had enough money to buy the necklace.

Jenny loved her pearls. They made her feel dressed up and mature. She wore them everywhere, Sunday school, kindergarten, and even to bed. The only time she took them off was when she went swimming or had a bubble bath. Mother said if they got wet, they might turn her neck green.

Jenny had a very loving daddy, and every night when she was ready for bed, he would stop whatever he was doing and come upstairs to read her a story. One night as he finished the story, he asked Jenny, "Do you love me?"

"Oh yes, Daddy. You know that I love you."

"Then give me your pearls."

"Oh, Daddy, not my pearls. But you can have Princess, the white horse from my collection, the one with the pink tail. Remember, Daddy? The one you gave me. She's my very favorite."

"That's okay, Honey. Daddy loves you. Good night," and he brushed her cheek with a kiss.

About a week later, after story time, Jenny's daddy asked again, "Do you love me?"

"Daddy, you know I love you."

"Then give me your pearls."

"Oh, Daddy, not my pearls. But you can have my baby doll. The brand new one I got for my birthday. She is beautiful, and you can have the yellow blanket that matches her sleeper."

"That's okay. Sleep well. God bless you, little one. Daddy loves you."

And, as always, he brushed her cheek with a gentle kiss.

A few nights later, when her daddy came in, Jenny was sitting on her bed with her legs crossed in Indian style.

As he came close, he noticed her chin was trembling, and one silent tear rolled down her cheek.

"What is it, Jenny? What's the matter?"

Jenny didn't say anything but lifted her little hand up to her daddy. And when she opened it, there was her little pearl necklace. With a little quiver, she finally said, "Here, Daddy, this is for you."

With tears gathering in his own eyes, Jenny's daddy reached out with one hand to take the dime store necklace, and with the other hand, he reached into his pocket and pulled out a blue velvet case with a strand of genuine pearls and gave them to Jenny.

He had them all the time. He was just waiting for her to give up the dime-store stuff so he could give her the genuine treasure. So it is, with our Heavenly Father. He is waiting for us to give up the cheap things in our lives so that he can give us beautiful treasures. (Unknown)

This story became much more powerful in our small groups in Kurdistan when people suddenly had the ability to actually accumulate "stuff." Unfortunately, it also made it glaringly evident that believers did not really trust that the treasure of their newfound faith in Jesus was strong enough to share. His incredible love for one's heart became that special pearl necklace that surely would be lost if freely shared with others. Viewed in the light of oppressed human nature, it was quite understandable, yet it was beyond tragic to watch.

Undoubtedly, at times I sorely missed the "wild west" type of atmosphere and remarkable "birth of hope" days that we had all experienced in 2004-2007. But despite the challenges and constant ambiguity, it remained a huge blessing to be living in the midst of it all and allowed to play a part for a time in what God was continually doing in this always unique and often absurd ancient land.

As the "glitter" of money and relative stability grew, interest in spiritual things and God's role in one's life continued to wane accordingly, as is so often the case around the globe. Everyone, including many of the believers themselves, was suddenly more concerned with governmental affairs and their own place in the proverbial sun. An exaggerated sense of victimhood and excessive entitlement even began to grow and spread within much of the recognized church leadership of the region. Sadly, money and material junk quickly became far more important than relationships or ongoing spiritual growth. This is no surprise to God, and He steadily continues the most important work of the Way through common struggling folk like me and you. It might not make today's headlines, but rest assured, it makes an eternal difference.

Without a doubt, the beauty of being here for almost two decades is that I now get to look back at the lasting gems that God produced through each and every individual who has come to serve Him. There truly are so many that I could not even begin to mention names, and God knows who they are anyway. I am only one strand in a mammoth and intricate tapestry of the Lord's design. I pray others will feel led at some point to share their own Kurdistan tale with the world as there is so much to rejoice over, despite the ongoing lack of huge revivals or obvious widespread conversions.

Over the years, I have interacted with over 20 different nationalities of faith-based workers here. The individual stories are rich and varied, but one clear thread runs through them all— "God told me to come." For example, there were two Iranian-American sisters in their sixties living here for years in a small town nearby. They had partnered with the Jesus Film folks and were doing whatever they could with what they had to help the people of Kurdistan find the same everlasting hope that dramatically changed their own lives many years ago as international college students in the USA. Over and over again, you hear the same kind of theme. Sadly, many also eventually leave with a sense of dejection, not really sure they made any difference in the bigger spiritual picture. In truth, though, every single line counts in God's design—it always has.

Undeniably, well-meaning people from the States frequently questioned my sanity in continuing here long-term, but God never wavers. Besides, it's actually not about location, which came as a great surprise when the Lord clearly told me it was time to leave Kurdistan. It's about listening and responding in obedience and trust regardless of how ludicrous it might seem to others. Eric Liddell, whose life and Olympic career were featured prominently in the movie *Chariots of Fire*, once said, "When I run, I feel His pleasure." I understand that well. To be honest, it is what keeps me going...or staying, depending on how you look at it. The Bible points out that without faith, it is impossible to please Him.[51] I would add that which I believe should be implied--with committed faith, you are able to not only please God, but you also delight His very heart!

***

Ironically, as physical circumstances continued to improve for most people in the Kurdish region, a powerful, "religious" spirit of fear was creeping in from many directions and ferociously attacking church leaders. Satan's "what if" scenario ruled their minds. Sadly, most did not recognize it as such and invariably searched for man's answers rather than God's provision. They were convinced that the only answer lay in the safety of abundant money and recognized power. When neither readily materialized, many leaders of all factions within the church decided that asylum-seeking migration was the only way to have the Christian life they had always dreamed of. Sadly, a mass exodus began then that has never truly ceased. Yet churches have continued to grow as they fill with Syrian refugees and Iraqi Christians from the south who find Kurdistan to be a blessed and peaceful haven after all they have been through.

Meanwhile, the regional government remained poised between wanting to be a model of democratic stability, religious freedom, and overall safety, while still facing the never-ending temptation of fraud and remaining vigilant to the possibility of approaching trouble. The secret, secret police began making more regular noise about the rising terrorist sleeper cells within the provinces. It is a fact that daily life in Kurdistan usually appears quite normal on the surface, and in general, no one realizes all that is continually happening behind the scenes until you are unexpectedly reminded.

One day a couple of American kids from a newly arrived family were simply videotaping the view from their own roof, when within minutes, an assortment of armed military men representing three separate countries showed up at the door demanding the footage. It turns out their roof faced a tree-covered hill that housed a covert military installation deep underground. Those sorts of unexpected incidents served as a sobering reminder that no matter what the carefree top layer of life looked like, immense malevolence still lurked right around the corner.

That overriding sense of nervous anticipation regularly created a more serious and stricter approach to the advent of holidays like Ramadan, the month-long fast of Islamic tradition. Suddenly, twice as many females wore head coverings, mosques were crowded, and a majority of the general population simply hid indoors during the daylight hours. As people seek spiritual renewal, the battle in the heavenly is always most obvious. Together with other like-minded organizations, we instituted our own version of the 24/7 prayer movement during the holiday, and believers reported amazing results from the practice. I found myself often unexpectedly involved in rich discussions about individual faith and how that is best lived out in one's everyday life.

Without a doubt, the ever-evolving thrill ride was seldom boring, often exhilarating, and occasionally a tad terrifying. All of which keeps you clinging to His hand. Daily quiet times are never optional, but rather essential for refueling. It was so thrilling to see our Iraqi students grab hold of this practice and run with it. I would often get phone calls at all times of the day and night as someone just had to share what God had just shown them. So often, it was the same truth He had just shared with me, and we rejoiced together in God's loving omniscience.

For myself, I am so grateful for the many, many authors that have taken the time to pen beautiful, scripture-laden daily devotionals that speak mightily to so many of us. My personal favorite remains the unique style of Sarah Young's *Jesus Calling: Enjoying Peace in His Presence,* as I resonate deeply with its structure, and so often, the relevant scripture references that are always offered pull me immediately into a deeper study of the Word:

DO NOT WORRY ABOUT TOMORROW! This is not a suggestion but a command. I divided time into days and nights so that you would have manageable portions of life to handle. My grace is sufficient for you, but its sufficiency is for only one day at a time. When you worry about the future, you heap day upon day of troubles onto your flimsy frame. You stagger under this heavy load, which I never intended you to carry. Throw off this oppressive burden with one quick thrust of trust. Anxious thoughts meander about and crisscross in your brain, but trusting Me brings you directly into My Presence. As you thus affirm your faith, shackles of worry fall off instantly. Enjoy My

Presence continually by trusting Me at all times…

But he said to me, "My grace is sufficient for you, for my power is made perfect in weakness." Therefore, I will boast all the more gladly about my weaknesses so that Christ's power may rest on me.

2 Corinthians 12:9 (NKJV)

Trust in Him at all times, you people; pour out your heart before Him; God is a refuge for us.

Psalm 62:8 (NKJV)[52]

Through the years, that message from the Lord has never changed. Don't be afraid! Just trust Me and focus on loving others well today. It was such ongoing solace to know that God's Spirit was right there with me…and actually wanted to be, even in the most mundane legs of the journey, not just when things got scary.

Prayerfully, in the beginning we as a mission, made the decision to be as overt as possible in our work here. The national believers also asked us to be, as it offered them a sense of legitimacy and international support. Thus, we never pretended to be anything but what we were—a

Christian mission organization focused on the biblical training of pastors and lay leaders. This put us as an organization in an ongoing tenuous and often exasperating position, but we also eventually gained a great deal of respect and confidence. Further, it allowed us to develop a number of lasting relationships with a variety of government officials who continue seeking truth in their own lives.

In the end, it took nine years of devoted prayer, a multitude of reports, verbal death threats, endless meetings, stern dressing-downs by various high officials, and lots of frustration to officially register Entrust as a legal entity for Church Leadership Training within the KRG. It was the first such organization of its kind to be formally recognized and a step that provided the KRG Council of Ministers with the ability to officially stand in support of alternative religions. The long-lasting president, Masood Barzani, even publicly declared before finally stepping down that Kurdish people should have the right to choose their own religion. He went on to explain that as an ethnic group, they were originally followers of Zoroastrianism before they were subjected to Islamic rule by force.

The registration was also an important step that benefited our Kurdish graduates in particular since it offered their new diplomas the legitimacy that they desperately needed; the majority had never been able to attend high school. Unfortunately, though, for many, it came to be viewed almost immediately as a sign of power and control rather than service, as well as a possible steppingstone for legal immigration to the West. As they put it, they could then become successful Christian leaders—just like the American teachers they so admired.

Entrust training was always meant to be based on a holistic three-part mandate of spiritual development—Bible Knowledge, Ministry Skills, and Character. The problem is that, of the three, only knowledge can be successfully imparted on a part-time or remote basis. The other two are a part of discipleship and take long-term hands-on dedication, particularly so when you are dealing with first-generation believers. Hence, one of the weaknesses of our program was that it quickly became primarily knowledge-based by default. Much information and precious nuggets of scripture were "rightly divided" in the quarterly intensives. But living it out in real-time regularly faltered as both of the other two facets were always meant to be "caught" rather than taught, and our overall residential presence was simply too sparse.

True, it is much easier now to stay in touch regularly than it ever was before the Internet. Unfortunately, it is not a worthy substitute for real life, as the virtual world is overwhelming and can be so easily manipulated. In my own mind, this is the reason that the Word still has to become flesh and dwell among the people, even in the 21st century.

Entrust colleagues, S & F, offered huge personal encouragement in that vein when they left established work in Greece to come and basically be the salt and light of Jesus day after day in the lives of the many struggling believers and leaders we worked with. S, as the freer male and an avid lover of fine beans, was quickly able to establish a kind of coffee shop evangelism that has actually proved to be one of the more ongoing fruitful avenues of reaching local people with the Gospel. His wife, F, was a special mentor and friend to the wives of our students, spending countless hours in their homes sharing recipes and learning "kitchen" Kurdish. To this day, those same ladies will tell you that her love and presence were life-changing for them in those years. I will always wonder what would have happened if several more families had followed their lead at that particular time. But, for reasons only God truly knows, those prayers were never answered in the affirmative.

Meanwhile, the horrible tentacles of the prosperity gospel, an idea that as a believer you deserve health, wealth, and happiness NOW, began to take root and sadly flourish in the hearts and minds of the baby Kurdish church. Unfortunately, it is not a concept strictly relegated to the developing world, as many western televangelists preach the same tune. It is definitely not a biblical concept, but it is certainly a much more "marketable" one from man's perspective than the idea of denying oneself and bearing a cross in Jesus' name.

It is not surprising, therefore, that early on in the competitive evangelical work of the Kurdistan region, an unfortunate practice I dubbed the "Jesus plus" mentality began and flourished. One Kurdish believer explained it this way:

> When the foreigners came, they told us about how much Jesus loved us and wanted us to be happy. They invited us to lovely conferences, and for some of us, it was the first time we had ever seen a bed or been served food by non-family members. It was amazing, and we loved our new friends and their stories. After a while, they told us we needed to be put down in the water to show we loved Jesus too and wanted to be with Him. Then they were so happy, and many of us got jobs from them.[53]

Money and missions are always a problem. In the developing world as a whole, there are gigantic, legitimate needs of every possible kind and never enough to go around. Further, in places like terrifying Iraq, it is often so much easier to throw money at a project and hope for the best than to invest significant blocks of one's own life.

Tragically, funding, no matter how generous, does not replace the ongoing need for full-time mentoring and accountability on the ground. Without such holistic support, the specters of jealousy, slander, corruption, exploitation, and avarice rear their ugly heads again and again. I have witnessed literally millions of dollars from well-meaning Christian sources wasted on projects in Kurdistan—many have never even been finished or used as intended. I have also seen much ongoing corruption from within churches and sending organizations as well as individual ministry leaders. It's nothing new. Paul addressed the same issue with Timothy:

The Lust for Money

These are the things I want you to teach and preach. If you have leaders there who teach otherwise, who refuse the solid words of our Master Jesus and this godly instruction, tag them for what they are: ignorant windbags who infect the air with germs of envy, controversy, bad-mouthing, suspicious rumors. Eventually, there's an epidemic of backstabbing, and truth is but a distant memory. They think religion is a way to make a fast buck.

Material wealth is always challenging. Add to that the ongoing present-day myth in the minds of many common people in most places that everyone in America is rich and has more money than they know what to do with. Thus, ongoing waste is to be expected. These days the ultra-rich in Kurdistan, like elsewhere, will routinely buy a perfectly sound house only to reduce it to rubble so that they can rebuild it exactly to suit their whims. Thus, the new novel idea that private individuals in America might actually make great sacrifices and go without to come to places in need because of their love for Jesus is simply not believed for the most part, at least for a while.

Moreover, a bloated sense of both ongoing persecution and subsequent entitlement has been a part of the autonomous region's mindset from its inception. Once the no-fly zone was created and a regional government was formed to serve the people, they immediately went about attempting to secure the lasting loyalty and love of the Kurdish people themselves by providing an excessive number of "government jobs" where few of the employees were actually expected to work. The leaders felt like the best way to gain allegiance, as well as the dependence of the people, was to completely take care of them.

In rural areas like Raparin, the decision was overly destructive as they took self-sufficient farmers and shepherds off the land and put them in offices where they did not have to really work anymore. Further, the misguided belief that physical work was a kind of punishment and should be avoided as much as possible quickly spread and permeated society. Over the ensuing years, new generations have not only lost the details of their history but also the know-how and practical abilities of trade and the agricultural skills needed to be fully independent. Worse still, a pervasive sense of extreme privilege leading to blatant dishonesty has infected the whole region. Sadly, I now believe a majority of the Kurdish people in Iraq would tell you that they do indeed deserve and desire independence. They just want someone else to pay for it.

***

Perhaps this is why Jesus never did ask us to make converts or leaders or even develop big programs to that end. When faced with such choices during His own earthly life, He routinely turned away and simply took the boys on another adventure in what it meant to be living with Him 24/7. It certainly did not mean adoring masses and 5-star accommodations; rather, just the opposite. There were crowds, to be sure, but they were there for what He could do for them rather than who He was, and He knew it.

Abundant life is found, not in glittery stuff, no matter its value, but in ongoing intimate fellowship with the Godhead. The greatest gift that the Lord has given me through the years in Kurdistan is the recognition that this truth has never altered. The more you need Him, the more He is there. He wants to be actively involved in every single second of our lives, but as the great Lover of our souls, he leaves the choice up to us and continues patiently tapping on each heart. That is His priority—yesterday, today, and forever.

Realize also that God has no money problems. He provides abundantly in His own ideal way and perfect time, which is almost always not the same as mine or yours. He loves you and me enough to give us what we need rather than what we want. Therein lies the rub. Look again at Jesus' time on earth—from birth onward, God never provided plentiful material support for His own Son. Instead, throughout the gospels, Jesus was continually forced to rely on others for simple room and board. That is not easy to accept from a human perspective. Satan regularly joins this "doubt-fray" as well, focusing on the strongest desire of the moment—just like he first did with Jesus on the mountain:

> *Next, Jesus was taken into the wild by the Spirit for the Test. The Devil was ready to give it. Jesus prepared for the Test by fasting forty days and forty nights. That left him, of course, in a state of extreme hunger, which the Devil took advantage of in the first test: "Since you are God's Son, speak the word that will turn these stones into loaves of bread." Jesus answered by quoting Deuteronomy: "It takes more than bread to stay alive. It takes a steady stream of words from God's mouth.*   Matthew 4:1-4 (MSG)

It is the same now. The Devil will constantly try to remind me that if God really wanted me doing what I am doing, He would provide amply, and physical life in general, as well as funding the ministry, would not be a constant struggle in uncertainty. However, the gospel accounts tell a vastly different story. Jesus was quick to point out in words and actions how easy it is for most to get distracted by the shiny cares of this world and miss the real gold of growing rapport with the Creator of the universe.

Sadly, people everywhere seem less and less willing to take such a risk these days. They are perpetually distracted on all sides by junk of various kinds and sizes. It is even easy to forget that we are still very much at war in the unseen world. Pastor and author John Piper deliberately use the phrase "wartime lifestyle" to remind himself and others of this unseen battle:

> It tells me that there are weapons to be funded and used, but that these weapons are not swords or guns or bombs but the Gospel and prayer and self-sacrificing love (2 Corinthians 10:3-5). And it tells me that the stakes of this conflict are higher than any other war in history; they are eternal and infinite: heaven or hell, eternal joy or eternal torment (Matthew 25:46).

> I need to hear this message again and again because I drift into a peacetime mindset as certainly as rain falls down and flames go up. I am wired by nature to love the same toys that the world loves. I start to fit in. I start to call earth "home." Before you know it, I'm

calling luxuries needs and using my money just the way unbelievers do. I begin to forget the war. I don't think much about people perishing. Missions and unreached people drop out of my mind. I stop dreaming about the triumphs of grace. I sink into a secular mindset that looks first to what man can do, not what God can do. It is a terrible sickness, and I thank God for those who have forced me again and again toward a wartime mindset.[54]

As the larger battle is primarily forgotten, interest and resources diminish accordingly. In my experience, even stable, ongoing funding for individual long-term ministry workers has dwindled significantly in the last couple of decades. Pastors frequently appear to view foreign mission work as competition and an almost superfluous financial drain with little return. Younger members of congregations are often not even aware of either the necessity or the blessing of a partnership in faith giving. Instead, they often literally voice confusion about why the sending organization is not paying its people.

Through the first half of the twentieth century, the boundary lines were much clearer. Well-funded mission organizations were formed to provide specific resources of all kinds and specialized training for the work ahead. International travel, for the most part, was neither quick, convenient, or even particularly safe. Missionary families often headed to the field with their belongings packed in coffins as they knew they would probably die sharing the good news of Jesus Christ in a faraway land. In fact, many did and left eternal, priceless legacies that will one day be fully revealed.

I personally do not know what the immediate financial answers are for places like Kurdistan, but God does, and He has made it clear to me not to be overly distracted from all that is so much more important. Occasionally I hear of interest from organizations with the capacity to invest in the human resource that is desperately needed, but so far, nothing has materialized. I regularly pray that, for their own sake, people will continue to go, serve, send others, and experience God at work—especially in those hard and broken places that the world has given up on, but He has not. As Jim Elliot reminded us all: "He is no fool who gives up what he cannot keep to gain that which he cannot lose."[55]

Chapter Nine: Dreams Die Hard

When you figure out you have it all wrong

I remember the change in his eyes most of all. I had just finished quizzing my dear friend, who was a top student, competent evangelist, and known house church leader. Shortly after the referendum fiasco (see Chapter 5, pg. 75-76), he had become more and more panic-filled, determined that the only solution to his problems was to leave the country with his family and seek asylum as a refugee. I asked him to tell me what it was he was looking for. His detailed response included a heartfelt need to protect his children, above all, and to find a happy, lasting place of health, peace, and safety. I listened carefully and then replied in earnest that it sounded like he was describing heaven. Suddenly there was a coldness in the room that was reflected in his eyes. "Heaven," a voice snarled in contempt, not sounding like my friend at all. I knew then that I had lost this particular struggle, but thank God that He never relinquishes control of the actual conflict for one's heart, even when it feels like it.

****

It was 4 AM on a cold and rainy day in February of 2018. I was numb from the shock of the most recent betrayal from within and operating on empty in every direction. Scheduled to return to the States for a much-needed break, I was rushing around to catch a taxi from the small town where I lived to the international bus station two hours away. As I sprinted down the stairs, electricity for the entire neighborhood went out, plunging the house into total darkness. At that moment, I tripped over a corner of the rug as I entered the kitchen and instinctively put my hands out to catch myself. I ended up inadvertently catching the handle of a boiling metal tea kettle and flipping it upside down onto my right thigh and feet. Struggling to disrobe, I went to the shower and plunged what I could into cold water. The flashlight revealed that the skin of my left instep had been completely sheered and now was rolled up at the bottom, while the network of veins and arteries lay naked before me. The other affected areas didn't look so good either. I knew my best chance of proper treatment and effective restoration was in my homeland. Hence, with continual prayers for protection from infection and that dazed state of autopilot that trauma produces, I wrapped the burns carefully, shoved them in oversized shoes, and headed out the door with tickets in hand for the three-day trip ahead.

Tension and fear had continued at an all-time high for months as Baghdad kept the Kurdistan airports closed to international travel. Thus, the best way out was the convoluted route of old. I faced a 15-hour bus ride from Erbil to Diyarbakir, Turkey, and then flew on from there to Ankara the next afternoon. The following morning, I finally boarded the international flight to Denver via Frankfurt, Germany.

Yes, there was constant pain, but those experienced with burns will tell you that third-degree burns don't hurt in the same excruciating manner that the less dangerous first-degree burns do because the nerves are basically dead. The mind-blowing agony comes later during the debridement process, prior to the actual skin grafting. By then, though, I was in the hands of renowned health care professionals at one of the top burn centers in the country just outside of Denver, Colorado.

It was a time of healing and repair while I battled the inevitable guilt of the unfairness of it all. Just because I was born with American citizenship, I could get the best medical help just by showing up, while so many of my friends back in Kurdistan suffered from illnesses and injuries of all kinds where the proper treatment is simply not available. In that scenario, even relatively minor problems turn major and actually become life-threatening. It is tragic and sobering to witness the ongoing injustices suffered by the general population in places like Kurdistan. Life is not fair, nor was the cross.

God does not play by our rules. He never has, and I am quite sure, thankfully, that He never will. Thus, I believe this life should be all about learning how to play by His. While we are besieged on all sides by wars of all kinds, pandemics, horrific natural disasters, and the increasingly real problems of finite resources, it is easy to imagine that the world is completely out of control. Especially with Satan badgering your conscience repeatedly with the hopelessness of it all. Frankly, one of Jesus' interactions that has always bothered me is when he calls the Apostle Peter "Satan."

From that time, Jesus began to show His disciples that He must go to Jerusalem, suffer many things from the elders and chief priests and scribes, and be killed and raised up on the third day. Peter took Him aside and began to rebuke Him, saying, "God forbid it, Lord! This shall never happen to You." But He turned and said to Peter, "Get behind Me, Satan! You are a stumbling block to Me, for you are not setting your mind on God's interests, but man's."

Matthew 16:21-23 (NKJV)

Poor guy, Peter was just trying to help and protect our beloved Savior. After all, Jesus had recently even renamed him the Rock upon which He would build his church. Which is it? As I prayed through this one with the Lord, He was clear that sometimes the truth is more important than any hurt feelings that may arise. What if Jesus had listened to Peter? Just think of what was at stake. No one is safe. Satan can and does throw random thoughts into our thinking, and he speaks through even one's closest allies, beloved family, or the occasional mission board. Be aware. Always check your motivation – man's interest or God's…?

In reality, God does not need our *help*. He simply wants *us*. We are His kids, and He enjoys us enough to offer an unbelievable opportunity to serve alongside Him as He salvages the world.

> *I don't think the way you think. The way you work isn't the way I work… For as the sky soars high above the earth, so the way I work surpasses the way you work, and the way I think is beyond the way you think. Just as rain and snow descend from the skies and don't go back until they've watered the earth, doing their work of making things grow and blossom, producing seed for farmers and food for the hungry, so will the words that come out of my mouth not come back empty-handed. They will do the work I sent them to do; they will complete the assignment I gave them.* Isaiah 55:8-11 (MSG)

Our job then must be to faithfully share those words through both actions and speech, trusting Him with the outcome. That is what He is asking. Life suddenly takes on new meaning. In Iraqi Kurdistan, it soon became apparent that to reach individual people with the good news meant wading through the divisive nature of two incredibly strong forces that continue to rule. I submit that both such ideologies originate from the pit of hell. One is the politics of religion that is quick to invade any congregation or leader that will allow it. Everything becomes about show, size, and influence. Divisions crop up over everything, and confidence in each other is lost. It is particularly difficult to avoid in an area like the Middle East, where religion is completely intertwined with government policy.

The other constant pull is the religion of politics, which continues to permeate the world as well. It's all about the "right" leader and platform… except it actually is not. Indeed, the two main political parties in the Kurdistan region continue to have a damaging chokehold on every aspect of society – both blaming all the problems on the other "side." Unfortunately, it is all the people have ever known with respect to a leadership model, and the infant church has been quick to follow, forming their own kind of legalistic, dictatorial party to run the church. In so doing, they effectively snuff out any idea of individual freedom in Christ without even realizing it.

***

Undeniably, as life quickly got progressively better for all, the temptation among believing leaders to seek power, prestige, safety, and, of course, money – lots of money – grew considerably. The majority became completely agenda oriented. They competed rather than cooperated, as the distrust and tension remained excruciatingly strong, constantly fueled by Satan himself.

Until I lived long-term in Kurdistan, I had always taken for granted the very special generational upbringing that Americans have been blessed with for centuries… at least until now. We were raised with the idea that we were one nation under God and have always been exceptionally fortunate and should give back out of our abundance. Moreover, steeped in the Judeo-Christian tradition, the founding fathers of the USA added purposeful twists to ensure the preservation of individual freedoms, with religious liberty being a priority. Like so many others, I grew up with a strong sense of pride and identity in this young country that rose to the top in a few hundred years, defying all odds. Kurds, on the other hand, grow up without such a sense of belonging or security. They have no understanding of the cost involved with patriotism, let alone its real value or eventual peril.

Unbeknownst to many Americans, patriotism is not a spiritual gift, and it can actually be a stumbling block to kingdom living. For me personally, the highlight of my family's own history was our part in the settling of the American West. I relished the idealistic and romanticized stories of settling the frontier. I was enamored with the story of the 12-year-old kid from Oklahoma who joined a wagon train along with his family and headed for the wilds of Montana. He would later become my grandfather, and I delighted in the tales that he and others from his generation often shared. Childhood play was often "cowboys and Indians" rather than "army", and it was not until years later that I realized my own racist guilt regarding the many indigenous tribes of the United States.

Lose the sentimentalized version, and one suddenly comes face to face with stark reality. They were there first, but we wanted it, so we took it in the name of civilization, no matter what the means. If we are brutally honest with one another, we have to admit that the American dream itself was built in part on bloodshed and terror. It just never seemed that way because we believed it was progress. Our forefathers were determined to build an independent Christian republic that would offer justice and liberty for all and eventually change the whole world for the better. Besides, we had the example of the Old Testament stories of God-ordained genocide to soothe our collective conscience as long as we did not think about it too hard. It was telling during the Entrust studies that our Kurdish students did not even like studying the Old Testament as they considered it too bloody and mean.

To be sure, what we as a nation did to the native peoples that were already on the continent, as well as to the ones we brought in to physically help build up the vision, like the Blacks and the Chinese, was simply wrong. But it still happened and cannot be undone, canceled, or erased. We should and are trying to tell individual stories and recognize the worth of specific clans and tribes. When I was a child, we called them savages, redskins, or Indians. Just in the last decade, we have finally stopped lumping them all together as the more politically correct "native Americans" and have begun to address them by their actual tribal names. USA road information signs now identify the original residents as Cherokee, Apache, Navaho, Blackfeet, Cheyenne, Salish, Flathead, and so on. In fact, as of 2020, 574 different tribes have now been formally recognized. It is an important, long overdue step, one that finally acknowledges the legacy of each individual tribe.

I now believe that the larger designation "Kurds" needs the same kind of "un-lumping," at least in an emotional and psychological sense. They are still very tribal in their thinking and have more loyalty to their own clans than to any government structure. They are already greatly divided by their different dialects and countries of residence, and nothing can be effectively achieved at this point by continuing to address it as simply "the Kurdish problem." Iraqi Kurdistan has had the best chance, among the Kurdish areas, of workable autonomy, and yet thirty years after the no-fly zone was established and an autonomous Kurdish government was formed, it remains exceptionally fragile, as they persist in being their own worst enemies. Long term, it is comforting to remember that in God's economy, it is never governments that matter, but rather the souls of individuals.

Absolutely, we were meant to dream. After all, we were formed in the very image of the Creator of the universe. Our innate ability to imagine and design is beyond description. Unfortunately, though, I have found that human dreams of grandeur, fame, and far-reaching influence, no matter how noble, have to die before the more important, eternal work can actually flourish in one's own heart.

After the five-year Bible program was concluded and Entrust was granted full legal status in the Kurdistan region, I prayerfully realized that any sense of a sole female head in the official church leadership arena would be detrimental. Moreover, the men desperately needed male mentors and friends who would be able to understand their daily struggles far better. Besides this, I was completely drained from pointless meetings, shameful politics, and rampant dishonesty everywhere. At the same time, the Spirit kept pointedly nudging me to focus on practical discipleship and find a way to live among and enthusiastically love ordinary Kurdish people.

Further, I was challenged by the idea that discipleship is not necessarily post-evangelism, especially in places like the Middle East, where so few have any real concept of who Jesus Christ actually is. How can we expect authentic mass conversions when they have never been introduced, much less given a chance to make a heart decision based on ongoing connection? Year after year, as faith-based organizations and residential workers, we talked about the various enigmas, held meetings and seminars, looked tirelessly for the latest and best programs, made massive, long-range plans, and yet…

Parable of the Fishless Fisherman

There was a group called Fishermen's fellowship. They were surrounded by streams and lakes full of hungry fish. Someone suggested they needed a philosophy of fishing. So, they carefully defined and redefined fishing and the purpose of fishing. They developed strategies and tactics.

Then they realized that they had been going at it backward. They had approached fishing from the point of view of the fisherman and not from the point of view of the fish. How do fish view the world? How does the fisherman appear to the fish? What do fish eat and when? These are all good things to know.

So they began research studies and attended conferences on fishing. Some traveled to faraway places to study fish with different habits. Some got PhDs in Fishology.

But no one had yet gone fishing.

So a committee was formed to send out fishermen. Since prospective fishing places outnumbered the fishermen, the committee needed to determine priorities. A priority list of fishing places was posted on bulletin boards in all the fellowship halls.

Still, no one was fishing.

A survey was launched to find out why. Most did not answer the questionnaire, but from those who did respond, it was discovered that some felt called to study fish, a few to furnish fishing equipment, and several to go around encouraging fishermen. What with meetings, conferences, and seminars, others simply didn't have time to fish.

Jake was a newcomer to the Fishermen's Fellowship. After one stirring meeting of the fellowship, Jake went fishing. He tried a few things, got the hang of it, and caught a choice of fish. At the next meeting, he told his story, was honored for his catch, and then scheduled to speak at all the Fellowship chapters and tell how he did it.

Now because of all the speaking and his election to the Board of Directors of the Fishermen's Fellowship, Jake no longer had time to go fishing.

Soon he began to feel restless and empty. He longed to feel the tug on the line once again. He cut the speaking, resigned from the board, and said to a friend, "Let's go fishing." They did, just the two of them, and they caught fish.

The members of Fishermen's Fellowship were many, the fish were plentiful, but the fishers were few. [56]

In short, I empathized with Jake. Around the same time, two major events fairly close together occurred in my stateside world of support. One was a heartbreakingly abrupt and horribly sad, high-level administration change within the mission organization that I had served with for over ten years. The other was a significant policy change within my home church that effectively eliminated financial support for individual message bearers. While I will always be thankful for their initial generosity, it made the immediate hit a huge one that went way beyond money.

I had to make a choice: go home for months of fundraising deputation without a clear vision of the way forward or find some source of income within Kurdistan that would allow me to pursue this new phase of the journey without delay. Within a few weeks, I discovered a posting for an English teaching job at a public university in Rania, the largest town in the rural district of Raparin. At the time, it was an easy decision as I had become certified in Teaching English to Speakers of Other Languages (TESOL) a few years prior, having seen the ever-increasing potential ministry value in such a service.

Many message bearers look at teaching English as an unnecessary bother that pays little dividend. Learners, on the other hand, look at it as a miraculous and sacrificial gift. Little did I know that God would use my new position so powerfully to continually change my thinking in a multitude of ways and mold me into a much better fit for His dominion.

***

The young man approached me shyly after class. We talked for a few minutes about his recent presentation. I could tell there was more on his mind, something that deeply troubled him. I watched him pause, clear his throat and fidget a bit as if he was mentally garnering his courage.

"I need to ask you a personal question, and I am not sure how. I mean, I love your class and all the new stuff we are learning about teaching English. You are a great teacher; it's just I have heard some stuff...and I need to know…"

He hesitated for a moment, and in the back of my mind, I prepared for the inevitable "Are you a missionary?" query, the response to which often feels like its own high wire dance in the dark. Thus, I was a bit taken aback when he suddenly squared his shoulders, looked me directly in the eyes, and said, "Please, tell me the truth – are you a spy?"

His question took me so off guard that I reacted with an amused bark. As I realized he was completely serious, I went on to reassure him that I was not now, nor ever had been a spy and would have made a horrible one. What an eye-opener with regard to the far-reaching tentacles of the religion of politics! I later learned that people in this area for centuries have believed that message bearers are actually agents of their home government's intent on further colonization.

Newshirwan Mustefa, a famous Kurdish writer and politician in Erbil, charged the missionaries with preparing the way for European domination of the region. "One of the tactics of the European countries to get a foothold in the [Assyrian] areas was to send religious missionaries."[57]

Newshirwan reviews the history of missions in the region and blames the French, American, British and Russian missionaries for operating on behalf of their governments. Consciously or not, Newshirwan says, missionaries gathered information and established a presence on behalf of their national interests.

> "Missionaries will deny that they were pawns of western governments or that Christians in Kurdistan were victims of mission power. However, Kurds saw it so, and in this case, perceptions made a new reality. "*58*

I also understand much better now why I was raised to believe that the American founding fathers immediately addressed the issue of the necessity for the separation of church and state. In truth, though, Thomas Jefferson was the first to use the phrase "separation of church and state" ten years after the constitution was ratified in a letter to a group of Baptists. In his letter, Jefferson cites the constitution's prohibition against the government establishing a religion or stopping any person from adhering to his or her beliefs. A vast majority of the founding fathers and signers of the Declaration of Independence and the constitution aligned themselves with Christianity and allowed their religious convictions to guide them in decision-making while in office.[59] Thus the idea of "separation of church and state" has been grossly misinterpreted and abused in modern-day America.

In short, I do not think that means we are supposed to stop wrestling with the value we place on the matter. Jesus's own advice to render unto Caesar what is Caesar's and unto God what is God's, coupled with His bizarre instruction to retrieve the tax money from the mouth of a fish,[60] relegates the importance of government mandates to a basic fact of life that should neither be ignored nor obsessed about.

Unfortunately, the concept of separation in itself is not a simple fix, especially when the founding ideologies generally adhere to a single religious tradition, such as Christianity in the USA and Islam in Iraq. Such core value systems or lack thereof are also going to control the key wealth of the area by default, which in turn regulates the government. Like it or not, generally, he who has the gold still makes the rules. Hence the theory of healthy separation and peaceful, fair cohabitation looks good on paper but stumbles regularly in real life.

***

Misguided, materialistic thinking further fueled the ongoing fraudulent selfishness, both in the government and among a majority of the people themselves within the region. The insatiable quest for more can never actually be satisfied.

The devil and his henchmen make sure of that on a daily, if not hourly, basis. Add the atrocious actions of the terrorist group known as ISIS, and it became a perfect storm – quick to shower heavy doses of fear and doubt that indeed God is actually not good and will take everything away at the slightest provocation and bring on pain, loss, and misery no matter how righteous you are. After all, let us not forget the hard lessons from scripture that whisper "no guarantees." Besides, who knows if eternity is even real… maybe it's just a nice story to keep us trying.

Since the question of heaven's existence was solved irrevocably for me when baby Johnathan gained entrance on April 26, 1992, I am always startled to find that many followers do not share my own sense of absolute certainty. For example, one of the requirements for field service with Servant Group International included an interview with a psychiatrist. The doctor's questions seemed innocuous enough at the time, and so I was surprised when the director called me in a few days later. He seemed a bit embarrassed to bring it up, but he needed my signature of acknowledgment. It turned out that the psychiatrist had put a possible red flag on my file following a particular response. He was mildly concerned from one of my answers that I might have suicidal tendencies.

The question was: "If you could go absolutely anywhere you wanted, where would you choose?" My response was instantaneous; to me, the answer is more than evident. Given such a choice, I would go to heaven. For the doctor, thinking of that sort was actually cause for concern. I found that both disappointing and troubling. It seems like we have lost our first love and the assurance that it nurtures. Since it is no longer politically correct in most "civilized" circles to talk about sin or hell's existence, we seem to have tragically misplaced the hope of heaven and God's own rule as well.

Furthermore, obedience does not necessarily equal "victory" as we know it. Without question, numerous magnificent people have ventured to places like Kurdistan, filled with a passion for doing something big for God. We all come with impressive aspirations and intricate ideas. In my own time here, I have met a multitude of earnest believers sacrificing much to share the love and life of Jesus with those who have never heard or seen. This is nothing new. It is what God asks for from each one of us for *our own* good in the basic training stage known as earthly life.

Robert Blinco, in his comprehensive dissertation *Ethnic Realities and the Church: Lessons from Kurdistan,* has provided the most extensive research to date on historical American missions in the wider Kurdistan region. He does not sugarcoat the story in the least but instead gives voice to the many faithful Christian workers who willingly forfeited so much, only to find themselves attacked and rejected time and again. To be sure, historically, Kurds were the bad guys when it came to the church, joining Turks and others in plunder, destruction, and often even killing foreign workers. This was tough to hear initially, as I also had the Kurds on a kind of idealistic pedestal right there with the ole US of A, both of which needed to be utterly shattered before I could actually be effective.

***

The Kurdish government was always very proud of the public record, maintaining that no American soldier had died on Kurdish soil during Operation Iraqi Freedom. Then in 2012, Jeremiah Small, a teacher at the Christian school where I had worked, was shot and killed in the classroom by a student who then turned the gun on himself. Jeremiah was thirty-three when he died and well-known for his passionate love for Jesus. His friends and students continue to honor his memory and impact a decade later. One day we will actually understand the why – just not yet.

Sometimes the task at hand is simply one of painful preparation, of moving boulders out of the way so tiny seeds can spout. Literally, for hundreds of years, message bearers have left everything behind to be obedient to God's call in difficult and isolated places, where they were often attacked rather than welcomed. What was the point? Oh, wait a minute, isn't that exactly what happened to God's own Son? Below are the lyrics to one of my all-time favorite hymns, entitled "It is Well with my Soul." The message of the song is made even more powerful when one learns the background:

This incredible story of faith belongs to Horatio Gates Spafford (1828-1888). Much like Job, he placed his trust in God during his life's prosperity but also during its calamities. A devout Christian who'd immersed himself in scripture, many years of his life were joyous. He was a prominent Chicago lawyer whose business was thriving. Horatio owned several properties throughout the city. He and his beloved wife had four beautiful daughters and one son. Life was more than good – it was blessed.

But faith, no matter how great, does not spare us from adversity. Just as Horatio hit the pinnacle of his profession and financial success, things began to change. It began with the tragic loss of their son. Not long thereafter, the Great Chicago Fire destroyed nearly every real estate investment Horatio owned.

Just a few years later, in 1873, Horatio decided to treat his wife and daughters to a much-needed escape from the turmoil. He sent them on a boat trip to Europe with plans to join them shortly after wrapping up some business in Chicago. Just a few days later, he received a dreadful telegram from his wife:

"Saved alone…" It bore the excruciating news that the family's ship had wrecked, and all four of his daughters had perished. As Horatio was on his way to meet his heartbroken wife, passing over the same sea that had just claimed the lives of his remaining children, it was then that he put his pen to paper, and the timeless hymn was born.

When peace, like a river, attendeth my
way,
When sorrows, like sea billows roll;
Whatever my lot,
Thou hast taught me to say,
It is well, it is well with my soul.
Tho' Satan should buffet, tho' trials
should come,
Let this blest assurance control,
That Christ hath regarded my helpless
estate,
And hath shed His own blood for my soul.

My sin – oh, the bliss of this glorious
thought-
My sin – not in part but in whole,
Is nailed to His cross, and I bear it no more,
Praise the Lord, praise the Lord, oh, my
soul.

And Lord, haste the day when the faith

shall be sight,

The clouds be rolled back as a scroll,

The trump shall resound, and the Lord shall

descend,

"Even so"- it is well with my soul.[61]

Many people, believers or not, will walk away from such a tale shaking their heads in utter disbelief. There is no way that any sane person could react positively to such a mammoth tragedy… Unless, of course, they, too, have experienced an excruciating level of personal pain and been met by God Himself in the midst of it all.

I know that it is one club that no one wants to belong to or wishes on anyone else. However, on the other end of such a sojourn, life begins to make sense in a way that it never had previously. It is what the apostle Paul meant in the 3rd chapter of Philippians when he talks about how loss is actually gain. Jesus suffered beyond description for us, and a hint of the same provides a sweet communion that nothing else compares to.

Then Jesus went to work on his disciples. "Anyone who intends to come with me has to let me lead. You're not in the driver's seat; I am. Don't run from suffering;

embrace it. Follow me, and I'll show you how. Self-help is no help at all. Self-sacrifice is the way, my way, to finding yourself, your true self. What kind of deal is it to get everything you want but lose yourself? What could you ever trade your soul for?"

Matthew 16:24-26 (MSG)

Throughout the ages, theologians have struggled with the concept of pain and why God continues to allow its existence in the lives of His beloved. Many scriptures deal with this incomprehensible theme and end with the realization that faith and active trust, no matter the situation, will always be more important from God's perspective than mortal understanding. Unfortunately, as Eugene Peterson points out, the world itself will never see it that way:

> We live in a time when everyone's goal is to be perpetually healthy and constantly happy... If any one of us fails to live up to the standards that are advertised as normative, we are labeled as a problem to be solved, and a host of well-intentioned people rush to try out various cures on us... The gospel offers a different view of suffering: in suffering, we enter the depths; we are at the heart of things;

we are near to where Christ was on the cross.[62]

***

Moving out to Raparin, in many ways, was like stepping back in time to the early days in Sulaymaniah. New dreams began to form. After almost ten years in the country, I had finally begun to learn to do nothing with such ambitions except to wait, pray and serve in love. People of the area were generally thankful for my presence and craved English training, which was the door to their career advancement in many areas. On the other hand, I was a kind of novelty as they had been isolated for a long time. Most had never met an actual follower of Jesus. Faith-based foreigners had been warned for years to stay away from the area as it was "known" to be a hotbed of religious extremism, guerrilla warfare, and Iranian control. I found the opposite.

The general population had obviously never received the hotbed memo and was refreshingly naive in so many ways. For instance, I taught with a number of Iranian Kurdish folk who routinely invited me to come home to Iran for a visit with them whenever we had a break. They were appalled to learn that, as an American, I was generally not allowed to enter their country, and it would be extremely dangerous to even try. I do not think they even believed me until they went home and spoke with various authorities who said the same exact things.

God's Truth cannot be found in either the religion of politics or the politics of religion, and I believe the day is coming when that will be most apparent. Jesus told us that He was going to prepare a place for us and that He would come back for us when the time was right.[63] That is the one and only dream to cling to and work for – the one that will not die and promises to result in that happy-ever-after beginning we all long for. If it were not so, He would have told us.

Chapter Ten: Eternal Treasure

Let go and Let God

Wherever God places or sends each one of us in this training life, we need to remember how much He values the uniqueness of each individual heart that He so lovingly designed and formed. I am sure that is why the increasingly popular pyramid marketing scheme mentality fails to work within ministry, though it is regularly attempted. Whether we realize it or not, that is what we are doing when our all-encompassing goal becomes such worthy refrains as "make disciples that make disciples." Even systematically focusing on unreached people groups, as noble as that sounds, does not seem to actually line up with God's own desires. The overarching agenda then becomes much more important than the individual relationship. From man's viewpoint, it certainly sounds like a great way to get the job done most efficiently and usher in God's rule once and for all. The problem is that it is not what Jesus actually told us to do and could well be the stern warning behind another Scripture (highlighting mine) that often gives me pause:

Being and Doing

"Don't look for shortcuts to God. The market is flooded with surefire, easygoing formulas for a successful life that can be practiced in your spare time. Don't fall for that stuff, even though crowds of people do. The way to life—to God!—is vigorous and requires total attention.

Be wary of false preachers who smile a lot, dripping with practiced sincerity. Chances are they are out to rip you off in some way or another. Don't be impressed with charisma; look for character. Who preachers are is the main thing, not what they say. A genuine leader will never exploit your emotions or your pocketbook. These diseased trees, with their bad apples, are going to be chopped down and burned.

Knowing the correct password—saying 'Master, Master,' for instance—isn't going to get you anywhere with me. What is required is serious obedience—doing what my Father wills. I can see it now—at the Final Judgment, thousands strutting up to me and saying, 'Master, we preached the Message, we bashed the demons, our God-sponsored *projects had everyone talking.' And do you know what I am going to say? 'You missed the boat. All you did was use me to make yourselves important. You don't impress me one bit. You're out of here.'*

"These words I speak to you are not incidental additions to your life, homeowner improvements to your standard of living. They are foundational words, words to build a life on. If you work these words into your life, you are like a smart carpenter who built his house on solid rock. Rain poured down, the river flooded, a tornado hit—but nothing moved that house. It was fixed to the rock.

"But if you just use my words in Bible studies and don't work them into your life, you are like a stupid carpenter who built his house on the sandy beach. When a storm rolled in, and the waves came up, it collapsed like a house of cards."

Matthew 7:14-27 (MSG)

Above all else, God cares about each one of us. Scripture is clear that He even knows about the life and death of each tiny bird that we ourselves readily discount as irrelevant.[64] Creation, too, repeatedly demonstrates the incredible attention God demonstrates in individual design. For instance, take a moment and think about how that delicious corn on the cob we all regularly devour was actually formed. I recently had a wise farmer explain to me that the hair-like silks that grow from the top of each ear and provide a source of grumbling for the preparer are, in truth, incredibly important to the final product. *Each* silken hair leads to a single potential kernel on the growing ear. If the silken strand has been pollinated, then a kernel forms from *each* strand, and *together* they form a delightful repast.[65]

One-on-one, remember. How can such be with our enormous population? The idea that God is actually big enough to be intimately involved with each one of us is truly mind-blowing. He would have to be all-knowing, all-powerful, and always with us in every second. Hmm, I guess that is one of the best descriptions of our almighty Father – omnipotent, omniscient, and omnipresent.

Moreover, I know the question many of us face when we try to explain God's goodness. If He genuinely cares *that* much, how could He allow literally millions of people to die from starvation every year or the horrific natural disasters that regularly wipe out thousands, or, or, or? Honestly, I have no idea. "Impossible!" shrieks our human brain in all its fragility, as God looks on and chuckles. His own perspective is so very different from ours. I know without a doubt that God laughs because I heard Him once at the most unexpected and seemingly inappropriate moment.

It was a beautiful blue-sky day, one of those rare occurrences in late summer that shows the beauty of rural Kurdistan at its breathtaking best. I felt terrific, having spent a refreshing weekend with DR, a long-time colleague who was also a single, divorced woman. She too had felt led as well to come to help out and share Jesus…for as long as it took. That particular morning, we enjoyed great coffee, an inspirational message, and a special extended time of prayer. I remember one of my favorite praise songs was on the radio as I cruised home.

Singing along, I had just turned onto the narrow two-lane highway that was thick with oncoming traffic. Without warning, I suddenly found myself staring at the flashing lights of a small, battered pickup barreling right for me. With all the traffic, my only real option was to plunge off the right side of the road in an attempt to escape. The embankment was fairly steep, and I slowed to keep control when the little menace caught the back end of my own truck and launched me into a single full roll. The seat belt worked perfectly, and as I made the 360-degree swirl, I heard a short, distinct laugh. In the end, no one was badly hurt, though both vehicles sustained major damage. Many dear friends have offered various explanations for the laughter, but to be honest, I am content with just the memory. All I know is that somehow it changed me in a positive way. Bad or good, nothing happens without His knowledge. Ever. Furthermore,

He is always able to do exceedingly, abundantly above all that we ask or think, if we just let Him.

* * *

Again and again, during the Kurdistan adventure, I asked our heavenly Father for direction, as both the brutal religion of politics and the evil politics of religion always seemed to win. Truly, no good deed went unpunished. The Lord's answer was always the same. Pray constantly, listen carefully, and faithfully love.

> *"I've told you these things for a purpose: that my joy might be your joy and your joy wholly mature. This is my command: Love one another the way I loved you. This is the very best way to love. Put your life on the line for your friends. You are my friends when you do the things I command you. I'm no longer calling you servants because servants don't understand what their Master is thinking and planning. No, I've named you friends because I've let you in on everything I've heard from the Father.*
>
> *"You didn't choose me, remember; I chose you and put you in the world to bear fruit, fruit that won't spoil. As fruit bearers, whatever you ask the Father in relation to me, he gives you.*

John 15:11-17 (MSG)

Hence, in August of 2013, I moved out to Rania, the largest town in the rural border region known as Raparin, to accept a position at the newly opened Language Center at the university. The University of Raparin primarily services a 35-mile-long front-range area at the base of the formidable Zagros Mountains that form a natural border between Iraq and Iran. The two largest towns in the area, Rania and Qaladze, are located at opposite ends of the stretch, and each houses a campus of the university. Sadly, as so often happens in the Kurdish administration, all the true decision-makers and top officials are at the larger Rania campus, so the Qaladza site is often viewed as an unimportant stepsister. Regrettably, this does nothing to unify the student body or create any sense of school spirit, the larger community, and belonging.

To make matters worse, all public universities in Kurdistan are assigned to one of the major political parties, which regulates management staff selection, financing, and policy of all kinds. What is good for politics is almost never good for learning. Higher education, at its best, should be a safe and inspiring place where free thought is protected and encouraged as people discover their adult identity and examine what they actually believe about everything. The young people of Kurdistan and elsewhere in today's world desperately need to be encouraged to consider life for themselves and make choices built on logic rather than a bloated sense of groupthink.

***

"Who ARE you?" the young Kurdish man seated toward the center of the classroom suddenly blurted out, effectively obliterating the uneasy silence that had settled over the other 25 or so students. The language center where I was employed is actually in Rania, and it was my first day teaching a conversation class to third-year English majors at the secondary Qaladze campus. All the students were Kurdish, and the vast majority were Muslim. Excited apprehension best described my own feelings as I entered the classroom and heard smatterings of plausible English. In the early years of my Raparin adventure, that was a fairly rare occurrence, and I was thrilled to think that these young people might actually be able to understand the basics. So, I looked back at the courageous youth in the soccer jersey with a grin. "I am pretty much an open book, what do you want to know?"

My response brought a smattering of nervous giggles since the class had recently studied the particular idiom I used. With that, the proverbial ice was broken, and we began an engaging game of introduction that further lightened the mood. Over the next year, we learned much from each other and had a great deal of fun in the process. With good reason, most of the girls were timid and shy, rarely speaking out in class and generally conceding to the obvious restrictions of a patriarchal culture. There were exceptions, though, and these intrepid females tended to gravitate toward me since, as a foreign woman in a position of authority, I was very much a rarity.

One courageous lass who was a bit older stood out among the others, having already taught successfully for a number of years before attending university. Her manner was reserved but friendly, and her hijab or head scarf was always perfectly placed without a single strand of hair escaping. She was brave, too, resolute in her determination to address the unfair treatment of women within Kurdish society. It made for many a lively class discussion as some of the other girls would follow her lead and dare to speak up themselves. Early on, she approached me after class with her own question.

"I love your class and your style of teaching. It is helping us all a great deal to learn these new methods and have a native speaker to interact with. I just have one question. What brought you out here to a place like Raparin?"

As I gazed into her inquiring eyes, I breathed a quick prayer: *Your words, not mine, Father,* and began to speak.

"Well, it might seem strange to you," I started, and then went on to surprise even myself. "To be totally honest, I believe that God asked me to come."

A soft smile lit up her eyes as she beamed. "I understand, and I am so very glad you listened."

Raparin was uniquely intriguing to me when I arrived. Almost the entire population of the area appeared to be Kurdish Muslim, though as time went on, I did come to hear of more than a few anomalies in both categories. However, those generally stayed silent and tried to blend in. People were shy but curious and most grateful that I had come to help.

As mentioned, the area had gained an infamous and undeserved reputation as a radicalized source for extremists and illegal smuggling. Thus, few Christian internationals even visited the area, despite its incredible beauty and friendly citizens. So, I was indeed an oddity, but people made me feel most welcome from day one. Undeniably, there are a few terrorist sleeper cells in the area, but they are quiet, known, and carefully watched. Before you gasp in horror, consider the growing reality that there might be such in your own neighborhood as well. It is the world we now live in. God's advice was and is always the same. *Trust me for today and cherish each individual heart I bring to you by letting Me love them through you.* Step by step, over and over, day after day. The shocker is that when you purpose to let God be fully in control, then miraculous connection starts happening without any sense of pushing.

I began to pray often for individual students as they came to mind. Four of them entered my thinking repeatedly as I sought the Lord's wisdom and guidance—the two described above and two other young men. All four slowly began to reach out in different ways and invited me to meet their families and spend time in their homes. Over the next several months, through such conversations and a variety of extra-curricular activities, a sense of community and trust was born within our small group. Three of them even arranged an all-day hiking picnic in the phenomenal Kandil Mountains above Qaladze. Over time, we formed a team; they were the interns, and I was the coach. Our numbers increased as we did life together, and it changed all of us.

We started talking about the necessity for a quality private English learning center in Qaladze. None existed there at that time. I introduced the platform of TESOL (Teaching English to Speakers of Other Languages) and the worldwide recognized certification process. The recent graduates were surprised to learn that language acquisition, particularly global English, is in no way purely an academic exercise. Thus, a standard university degree in English does not fully prepare you for either triumph in teaching other non-native speakers or effective communication in your target language in daily life.

Therefore, the original four interns, followed quickly by about ten others, enrolled in and successfully completed a reputable online TESOL certification course of over 150 hours. They found the course overall to be difficult and challenging but exceptionally useful in practical methodology, full of new material that they had never studied at the university. Our first year of adult classes in 2015 was quite successful. We followed that with a fabulous kid's program in the summer of 2016, which we were able to maintain and steadily grow for three years until 2020, when Covid 19 shut everything down.

Unfortunately, even with the youth, it was always a struggle to get adequate funding. Quality English instruction has never been economically sustainable in the rural private sector since people expect the government to provide it for free. Likewise, it has become apparent to me over the last few years that the government is no longer sure that such training for the general public is in the regime's own best interest. They have made it clear that they are definitely no longer willing to pay for it. Perhaps they have begun to realize that when common people are able to communicate in a worldwide language, it allows them their own sense of "voice" outside Kurdistan, and that can be fatal for a dictatorial dynasty-type rule. Unfortunately, the people themselves have yet to understand the implications of this new thinking.

When the government imploded during the ISIS peril, the general public complained loudly but made no alternative plans. Truly, I believe many people in rural Kurdistan now actually have the financial capacity and might pay a premium price for a school filled with American teachers. However, such schools are unrealistic because of security and infrastructure requirements, as well as the overall cost involved. Complicating this picture is the fact that formal education has never become a recognized core value of the general population here. It remains much more crucial in many minds, both Christian and Muslim, to fight continually for one's "rights," even at the expense of their children's futures.

Those who did feel differently were the ones, regardless of their religious affiliation, who were attracted to the work of our non-profit organization that focused on Holistic Education and Community Development. We talked about and tried different ways to slowly change the deeply entrenched faulty thinking patterns. We were often frustrated by a badly broken system, but we learned to rejoice in small victories and continued seeking ways to make a difference. Most importantly, we became a kind of family that allowed these young Kurdish people to begin to understand and enjoy community with people they were not related to but with whom they share common goals and interests. Spiritual matters were often discussed in private. Christian visitors regularly came to help, freely shared their faith, and actively showed how such is worked out in daily life. Incredible seeds were planted in these young people's minds. They also discovered to their own delight, that they actually do have the ability to think for themselves, disagree with one another and yet still be friends. Many of the team over the years openly expressed that such lessons couched in the undeniable love of God profoundly altered their lives for the better.

As I was leaving, F and company hosted a farewell meal. I appreciated all of the assorted accolades from the Raparin team, but one stood out and affirmed for me that the message had been delivered:

> The thing about Kath that changed us all from
> day one was that she didn't care whether you
> were black, white, yellow, Muslim, Christian,
> smart or dumb – she only cared that you knew
> that God loves you deeply, and because of
> that we could risk loving each other. Before
> she came, we would never dream of hanging
> out with people from other towns, even in our
> general vicinity, as they were "others,"
> strangers not to be trusted. Now look around
> this room – there are people from every town
> in Raparin and beyond. We are now like a

special family that loves each other, and our lives will never be the same. That was the thing about Kath. God bless you, Lady.

***

So what lies ahead? The world is messy, sad, and literally bursting at the seams when we look at sustainable survival. We have been warned by the Lord for ages that enormous troubles were coming to the whole planet. When the disciples asked Jesus about the timing, His reply was telling:

Later, as he was sitting on Mount Olives in full view of the Temple, Peter, James, John, and Andrew got him off by himself and asked, "Tell us, when is this going to happen? What sign will we get that things are coming to a head?"

Jesus began, "Watch out for doomsday deceivers. Many leaders are going to show up with forged identities claiming, "I'm the One." "They will deceive a lot of people. When you hear of wars and rumored wars, keep your head and don't panic. This is routine history, and no sign of the end. Nation will fight nation, and ruler will fight ruler, over and over. Earthquakes will occur in various places. There will be famines. But

Mark 13:1-8 (MSG)

He goes on to explain that it is actually going to get much, much worse before it gets eternally better. Again, nothing in the world surprises God, and that is a reality that no human can fathom. While it is so easy to grow increasingly concerned to the point of panic, we must circle back to the massive reminders in Scripture not to be afraid. This is the step of faith that makes all the difference.

Instead, though, believers often jump to what might best be described as a heavenly get-out-of-jail-free card. Any discussion of Armageddon, the horrific, final battle between good and evil that is predicted in the Bible, often provokes the rather flippant response of "Sure, glad I am saved. I don't have to worry about that, as I will be gone before the real trouble starts."

I find that attitude extremely distressing. They are referring to what is known as the rapture, an event also described in Scripture when Jesus Himself returns to snatch the faithful away before the worst of the horrific ending known as the tribulation. Many theologians believe this rapture will happen prior to the advent of the tribulation period, effectively rescuing God's own from the abysmal fury. Still, there is always the possibility that the scholars are wrong, and He may well have a unique plan that we have yet to even conceive of. Meanwhile, I am convinced that I need to keenly trust Him *no matter what,* unreservedly share His love, and stay focused on active preparation for the Kingdom life ahead. Praying continually and expectantly is essential in getting on with the business of joining in God's harvest, another important picture scripture paints of the process.

In my twenties, I was involved in various agricultural endeavors for a number of years. However, the true demands and consuming nature of the "harvest" did not become a reality to me until I found myself helping to manage a 1,000-acre hay ranch in far northern California for a few years. When there is much at stake, harvesting becomes all-important. Everything else in one's personal life has to take a secondary role. Timing, focus, and unwavering commitment are absolutely essential to a successful outcome. There is a short window of time when the "crop" is at its premium value, and it's almost never at a convenient moment. The sacrifice and pain rapidly dim though, as the whole harvesting team experiences a tremendous sense of satisfaction and accomplishment when that last bale of premium hay is successfully stacked in the barn.

To harvest, in the spiritual sense, is to equip and encourage others to be purposeful followers in a growing relationship with God Himself. Indeed, the Lord uses this picture of the harvest, agriculture's ultimate payoff, on many occasions. It is exactly what Jesus did with the twelve during his earthly life of ministry. It is important to remember that they are meant to be His disciples, not yours or mine. We just bear His message.

We can only imagine the joy and triumph that awaits, as He promised, on that day when the yield is finally complete. As the work in Kurdistan swirled on, I must admit that I often longed for the tidy, measurable fields of that hay ranch, but such is not God's way. I believe that is because He wants our obedience firmly entwined with an overwhelming sense of utter dependence. Notice the context preceding the harvest statement in Matthew 9. Jesus had *just finished* raising the dead, healing the sick, giving sight to the blind, and speech to the mute:

> *Then Jesus went about all the cities and villages, teaching in their synagogues, preaching the gospel of the kingdom, and healing every sickness and every disease among the people. But when He saw the multitudes, He was moved with compassion for them because they were weary and scattered, like sheep having no shepherd. Then He said to His disciples, "The harvest truly is plentiful, but the laborers are few. Therefore, pray the Lord of the harvest to send out laborers into His harvest."*

Matthew 9:35-38 (NKJV)

Clearly, the fabulous teaching and awe-inspiring healings for all were never of final importance to Jesus. He always saw beyond the "show" to the heart issues that seemed to break his own. In too many instances, potential ministers in Kurdistan are just like those sheep. They are already captivated by the person of Jesus, but they feel alone and frightened, unsure of what they should do with this newfound relationship, struggling to survive in obscure nooks and crannies throughout this hostile region.

For obvious reasons, the harvesting work becomes inordinately labor intensive in such an environment. The effective harvester has to be part teacher, part servant, part facilitator, part billy goat, part counselor, part coach, part mediator…and on goes the list. Hence the need for more workers is without limit. The situation is truly hopeless and always has been without the reality of Jesus Christ and the ultimate price that he already paid to conquer death forever.

That was the ongoing gift of Kurdistan. Life in such a place is so relentlessly edgy and uncertain that detailed planning for the future generally seemed to be an unending exercise in futility. This regularly causes great angst in the faith-based corporate world of the new millennium. Regardless, it is what it is, and to pretend otherwise, especially for funding purposes, would be dishonest. In time, I realized that such is a blessing in disguise as it continually draws one back to the Master:

This is also the most unexpected blessing of the recent pandemic that I continually hear expressed on both sides of the ocean. It has provided a massive reset regarding the priority of family relationships. We are suddenly not too busy to be actively involved with each other, and that has improved many lives. The connection has always been God's priority. Consider the existence of the inexplicable Trinity. Regardless of how such a paradox regularly causes controversy and befuddles even the most brilliant, still, taken on faith, it remains a piercing illustration of a relationship in perfection as the ultimate three-in-one. Moreover, He pleads for us to discover the *same* level of intimacy with each other, as that alone will change the world. [66]

Once again, if such were not possible, why would a loving God ask us to do it? He admonished us repeatedly to live for Him by giving ourselves away. Then He went on, throughout his worldly life, to demonstrate exactly what he meant. We lose something incredibly vital unless we experience Jesus as a living, breathing, three-dimensional human reality rather than a philosophical theory. Author John Eldredge offered just that when he delved into the Gospel accounts and wrote the inspiring book *Beautiful Outlaw: Experiencing the Playful, Disruptive, Extravagant Personality of Jesus.*

Late into the night, early in the morning, walking down the road, in the middle of his supper, at home, abroad, Jesus offers. His time, his words, his touch, flowing like the wine at Cana. To appreciate the reality of it all, remember, this is not Superman. Remember his loneliness, his weariness, his humanity. This is utterly remarkable – particularly in light of the fact that this is a man on a life-or-death mission. He is lavish with himself.

And that's the key, right there – that giving of himself. That is what is so precious. Moses offered leadership and tirelessly. Solomon handed out the rarest of wisdom free of charge. Pilate seemed willing to toss to the crowds anyone they wanted. But Jesus gives himself. That is, after all, what he came to give, and what we most desperately need.[67]

Personally, He keeps telling me to lighten up. Go on a picnic or walk on the beach. Reflect on His goodness and actively share the only source of hope. Always remember that it takes conscious, sustained prayer and effort to keep the Lord in full control of one's life. Yes, this fallen world is an absolute disaster. Yes, Armageddon is on its way, just as it has been since He told us about it way back when. The pressure's off, though. It's not about me…or you. Instead, it's all about the One who is coming back to set things right forever.

Think about Jesus's last days on earth following the crucifixion. He had literally just been to hell and back when we find Him in the midst of a rather amusing game of divine hide and seek followed by a "simple" breakfast-on-the-beach reunion with the boys. What?!? Shouldn't there be massive thunder and lightning – maybe an earthquake or two? Wouldn't there be huge parades and prostrate worshipers abounding with grave admonitions offered in unearthly tones for the disciples' various recent failures at the cross?

Apparently not. When Jesus uttered the final words, "It is finished," that is what He meant. When God ripped the temple's holy veil of separation from top to bottom, He did not decide later to sew it back up. Access to the Almighty was forever established through the blood of His Son. That is the best news of all. Isn't it worth going out of your way and comfort zone to communicate with those who have never heard?

Take a chance on God that radically alters your life. I believe that the Lord is asking each one of us to live a life of spiritual abundance here and now by consciously embracing Him and loving one another with His strength. Beware, your closest friends and allies may not understand right now, but one day they will, so do it anyway. Graduate with honors. Cherish, nurture and enjoy the relationships that He entrusts to you, who or wherever they are. Follow His lead. Be generous. Give yourself away to those He shows you. Do not be afraid; just be alert and watchful as you pray through each day. Talk it all out with Him, and then listen carefully as He will show you exactly what to do at the precise moment you need to know. For now, just open that door and take time to refresh in His presence. Appreciate His creation as you steadily get to know Him better and introduce Him around. After all, we are going to live together eternally so we might as well get used to one another.

That is my story, and I am sticking to it…

what's yours?

Notes

Introduction

---

[1] Ryan Shaw, *Waking the Giant* (William Carey Library, 2013), 144

Chapter One
[2] With God's help, Entrust' s accessible mentoring program, coupled with a quality curriculum, has produced thousands of maturing male and female leaders in Eastern Europe and the former Soviet Union. A number of these former students are now leading healthy congregations and teaching others to do the same just as the apostle Paul charged Timothy: "And the things you have heard me say in the presence of many witnesses entrust to reliable people who will also be qualified to teach others." 2 Tim 2:2. www.entrust4.org
[3] *The Other Iraq*—DVD Kurdistan Development Corporation 2005
[4] The natural birth is referred to as the emblem of the new birth (Jn 3:3-8; Gal 6:15; Ts 3:5, etc.)
[5] John 21:15-19

Chapter Two
[6] Romans 8:16
[7] Iraqi Kurdistan "Population and Demographics" https://www.wikipedia.org Sept 2007
[8] Mike Tucker, *Hell is Over: Voices of the Kurds after Saddam* (Lyons Press, 2004), 9
[9] Iraqi Kurdistan "Iran-Iraq War and Anfal Campaign"; https://www.wikipedia.org Sept 2007
[10] C.S. Lewis, *God in the Dock: Answers to Questions on Christianity* (Eerdmans Publishing, 1970), 5-52

Chapter Three
[11] Kevin McKiernan, *The Kurds: A People in Search of their Homeland* (St Martin's Press, 2006)
[12] Christiane Bird, *A Thousand Sighs, A Thousand Revolts* (Random House, 2004) 7
[13] Jerry B Jenkins, *Writing for the Soul* (Writers Digest Books, 2006) 30-31

Chapter Four
[14] John Eldredge, *EPIC: the story God is telling* (Thomas Nelson, 2004)101-102
[15] https://www.jesusfilm.org

[16] ION is an affiliation of agencies and organizations working together with the common goal of making God's Word available to oral communicators in culturally appropriate ways that enable church planting movements everywhere. The International Orality Network is part of the Lausanne Movement and grew out of the Lausanne Committee for World Evangelism in 2004. ION has since grown to be a global network of over 2,000 organizations. https://www.orality.net

[17] 1 Corinthians 2:14 *The person without the Spirit does not accept the things that come from the Spirit of God but considers them foolishness, and cannot understand them because they are discerned only through the Spirit.* (NIV)

[18] Gospel of John the – 4th chapter tells the story and discourse between Jesus and the Samaritan woman.

[19] https://www.brainyquote.com/quotes/peter_marshall_392737

[20] 1 Corinthians 7:8 *I do, though, tell the unmarried and widows that singleness might well be the best thing for them, as it has been for me. But if they can't manage their desires and emotions, they should by all means go ahead and get married. The difficulties of marriage are preferable by far to a sexually tortured life as a single.*

Chapter Five

[21] http:/www.robertburns.org/works/97.shtml

[22] Paul Borthwick and Ferni B. Adeleye, *Western Christians in* Global *Mission: What's the Role of the North American Church?* (*InterVarsity* Press, 2012) KL 916-923

[23] ***BEKAS*** film: ASIN: B01CYDL4XW; Format: Import, PAL, Subtitled, 2012

[24] Kawa Ahmed Abdullah; Tea house, Salim Street Sulaymaniah; April 28, 2006

[25] "The 1991 Iraqi Uprising - Kurdish Raparin Documentary" (Everything About Kurdistan, 2000) https://www.youtube.com/watch?v=sNwNAi8CFzw

[26] CNBC 25: Ben Bernanke and Alan Greenspan

[27] Stephen Mansfield, *The Miracle of the Kurds; A Remarkable Story of Hope Reborn in Nothern Iraq* (Worthy Publishing 2014) 76

[28] https://2wkblog.com/2017/11/03/are-you-a-circular-or-a-linear-thinker   2/kim hudson 2017

[29] Nazanin Soz Rasul Newroz celebration, Massef, Erbil Iraq March 24, 2011

[30] Groupthink is a mode of thinking in which individual members of small cohesive groups tend to accept a viewpoint or conclusion that represents a perceived group consensus, whether or not the group members believe it to be valid, correct, or optimal. Groupthink | psychology | Britannica

[31] The Navigators is a ministry that shares the gospel of Jesus and helps people grow in their relationship with Him through Life-to-

Life® discipleship, creating spiritual generations of believers. Since its founding in 1933, The Navigators has upheld the mission "To know Christ, make Him known, and help others do the same®."
https://www.navigators.org/about/

32 Nabeel Jabbour, *The Crescent through the Eyes of the Cross: Insights from an Arab Christian* (NavPress,2014) Kindle locations: 410,418,425

Chapter Six

33 Isaiah 55:8,9 *"For My thoughts are not your thoughts, Nor are your ways My ways," says the LORD. "For as the heavens are higher than the earth, So are My ways higher than your ways, And My thoughts than your thoughts.* NKJ

34 Much Ado About Gender Roles | Christianity Today

35 https://www.franciscanmedia.org/jesus-extraordinary-treatment-of-women/

36 As punishment for his disobedience and the grave dishonoring of his angelic post, God cast Lucifer out of heaven by hurling him and his army of fallen angels to Earth (Isaiah 14:15; Ezekiel 28:16-18; Revelation 12:9) and condemning them ultimately to hell (Matthew 25:41). Why was Lucifer, Satan, Cast out of Heaven? (crosswalk.com)

37 CS Lewis, *Screwtape Letters Annotated Edition* (New HarperOne, 1961) 65

38 https://www.theguardian.com/society/2014/feb/06/what-is-female-genital-mutilation-where-

39 https://www.studyfinds.org/men-women-brains-different

40 Nik Ripken, *The Insanity of Obedience, Walking with Jesus in the Tough Places* (B&H Publishing; Nashville, Tennessee 2014) 82

Chapter Seven

41 John 4:5–42=Samaritan woman; Mark 5:1–20=Demonic of Gadarenes; Luke 7:1–10=Roman Centurion; Matthew 15:21-28=Canaanite woman.

42 Jayson Georges, *The 3D Gospel::Ministry in Guilt, Shame and Fear Cultures*(Time Press 2017)Introduction

43 Jayson Georges, *The 3D Gospel::Ministry in Guilt, Shame and Fear Cultures*(Time Press 2017) 12-13

44 Samuel Coker Holdsambeck; Alabama; February 2022

45 Max Lucado, *A Gentle Thunder* (2001 Upwords, May 17, 2020) 22

46 Bible.org *Jesus' encounters with religious leaders versus the encounters of Jesus with others* - Jesus often clashed with the Jewish religious leaders. They were the leading citizens – yet Jesus criticized them and exposed their hypocrisy. This is in contrast to his treatment of women, tax collectors and leprosy sufferers. These people were often regarded as second-class citizens, but Jesus makes a point of treating them as equals.

47 Luke 24:21; Acts 1:6
48 Can Satan Read Our Minds and Know Our Thoughts?
(learnreligions.com)
49 Ephesians 6
*Finally, my brethren, be strong in the Lord and in the power of His
might. Put on the whole armor of God that ye may be able to stand
against the wiles of the devil.*
*For we wrestle not against flesh and blood, but against principalities,
against powers, against the rulers of the darkness of this world, against
spiritual wickedness in high places. Therefore, take unto you the whole
armor of God, that ye may be able to withstand in the evil day and,
having done all, to stand.*
*Stand therefore, having your loins girded about with truth, and having
on the breastplate of righteousness,*
and your feet shod with the preparation of the Gospel of peace.
*Above all, take the shield of faith, wherewith ye shall be able to quench
all the fiery darts of the wicked. And take the helmet of salvation and
the sword of the Spirit, which is the Word of God, praying always with
all prayer and supplication in the Spirit, and watching thereunto with
all perseverance and supplication for all saints.* NKJ 6:10-18
50 Joel C Roseburg; *Inside the Revolution* (Tyndale House Publishers,
2009) 395

Chapter Eight
51 Hebrews 11:6 *And without faith it is impossible to please God,
because anyone who comes to him must believe that he exists and that
he rewards those who earnestly seek him."* NIV
52 Sarah Young, (Thomas Nelson, 2004) 206
53 Kawa Qadir; Sulaymaniah Cultural Center 2005
54 John Piper, *Don't Waste Your Life (*Crossway Publishing, 2009) 111-
112
55 Elisabeth Elliot, *Through Gates of Splendor* (Tyndale Momentum,
1981) 127

Chapter Nine
56 Parable of the Fishless Fishermen | Cru
57 Newshirwan 1992:260).quote from Ethnic Realities (below)
58 Robert Blincoe, *Ethnic Realities and the Church: Lessons from
Kurdistan,* (William Carey Press, 2018) Chapter 3 kindle position 1747-
1754
59 https://www.compellingtruth.org/separation-church-state.html
60 Matthew 17:24-26
61 https://www.godupdates.com/story-behind-it-is-well-with-my-
soul/#who-wrote-it-is-welsoul_March, 2016

[62] Eugene Peterson, *A Long Obedience in the Same Direction: Discipleship in an Instant Society* (Downers Grove IL: University Press 2000) 138

[63] Gospel of John; Chapter 14

Chapter Ten

[64] Matthew 10:29-31 *Are not two sparrows sold for a penny? Yet not one of them will fall to the ground outside your Father's care. And even the very hairs of your head are all numbered. So don't be afraid; you are worth more than many sparrows.* NIV

[65] https://www.davesgarden.com/guides/articles/view/4341/

[66] John 17:21-23 *I pray also for those who will believe in me through their message, that all of them may be one, Father, just as you are in me and I am in you. May they also be in us so that the world may believe that you have sent me. I have given them the glory that you gave me, that they may be one as we are one— I in them and you in me—so that they may be brought to complete unity. Then the world will know that you sent me and have loved them even as you have loved me.* NKJ

[67] John Eldredge, *Beautiful Outlaw: Experiencing the Playful, Disruptive, Extravagant Personality of Jesus*(Yates &Yates, LLP 2011) 64